Homo Habilis

My Tanzanian Adventure

Karl Aston

*To Emily,
Best wishes, Karl.*

Published by New Generation Publishing in 2021

Copyright © Karl Aston 2021

First Edition

ISBN: 978-1-80369-981-3

www.newgeneration-publishing.com

New Generation Publishing

Foreword

My story is based on some of my personal memories of a trip to Tanzania at the beginning of nineteen-ninety. Whilst the events are how I remember them, the names of my characters have been changed and, therefore, do not truly represent the other people with whom I travelled. However, I hope it highlights the excitement, fun and beauty of my trip, as well as the danger, sadness and inevitability of life in the wilderness. I met some amazing people along the way, especially the tour leader and his friends, as well as our wonderful drivers, who were also our guides.

I started to write the story at the beginning of the new millennium, and was encouraged by my mother to write it in the "first person". Sadly, she died of cancer four years later, before I had finished the book. I also have cancer now, and during the past year I have had the motivation to complete my story, and publish it in her memory, donating any profits to cancer charities.

I, therefore, dedicate this book to my mother, Olive. I also give my thanks to Janet and Julia for all their help and encouragement in completing the book. All photographs and illustrations are my own creations, with help from my electronic pencil.

I hope you enjoy reading this story, and I hope it will encourage you to write your own.

Happy reading

Karl Aston

Introduction

It was a wet evening, towards the end of January nineteen-ninety, in the Kilimanjaro Region of Northern Tanzania. I could hardly believe it because there I was in Marangu Safari Lodge, looking out of my window in awe at the beautiful garden, and snow-covered Mount Kilimanjaro over in the distance, with Mount Meru close by. However, because of the light rain and evening sunshine, the mountains were only just visible in the distance.

The Lodge, situated about fifty miles from Arusha town, was set in a beautiful subtropical garden. Looking out I could see, through the light rain, a glimpse of sunshine reflecting on the garden. There were red flowering shrubs in the foreground and larger green trees behind, setting the scene for the sheer magnificence of the mountains.

I was there with an animal and bird watching tour, as the result of a local advert to make up the party numbers. I was sharing with a gentleman named Russell Green, whose wife was unable to join the tour. I met him for the first time at Heathrow airport, but I had met Tom Smith, the Tour Organiser, at an inaugural meeting to obtain the details prior to this trip.

Looking out of the window was a fabulous introduction to what was going to be an interesting and exciting adventure. I felt lucky that I had the opportunity to experience this tour, something I had always wanted to do since childhood. I have always had a love of animals and birds although, I must point out, I was not familiar with tropical species of birds. Therefore, I was looking forward to seeing some of them. I had visited zoos all my life, but had never had the opportunity to pursue that sort of tour before. I was particularly looking forward to seeing the "big five" animals, the Lion, Leopard, Rhinoceros, Elephant and African Buffalo. There were others on my list, like the Cheetah, if I was lucky to see one. I believed they were quite elusive. Even so, I was also excited to see the birds and reptiles as well, particularly Birds of Prey and Crocodiles, which fascinated me.

Resting there was a welcome relief, following the long day up near the Kenyan Border looking for wildlife. However, my personal adventure really began with my journey from York, travelling the four and a half thousand miles to Kilimanjaro.

I first travelled to London from York by train, arriving there at around lunchtime. It was quite sunny when I arrived in the capital, so I decided to have a look around the stores in central London, prior to catching the underground to Heathrow Airport, where I met the other tour members. I bought a couple of tapes, and a headset for my portable cassette recorder, from a music mega store on Oxford Street, and slotted them into my large, light blue holdall. This I had bought in York especially for the trip. It was padlocked so I put the tapes into the side zip pocket. I had bought a copy of Simon and Garfunkel's Greatest Hits, and one of my favourite Shadows albums, because I thought they would help to pass away the long evenings in Africa, when it was dark and I had nothing else to do. This was not to be. They disappeared somewhere between Heathrow and Kilimanjaro, from my unlocked zip pocket. Another lesson in reality learnt, and I hoped that whoever had taken them was enjoying the music. At the same time, I bought two blank audio tapes on which to record my adventure. These I had put in my coat pocket, and thankfully were still with me.

After a snack in central London, I made my way, as instructed, to Heathrow Airport by Underground. I was met by Tom Smith, a tall man roughly my age, the Tour Organiser. Tom introduced me to his friend, Robert Jones, a shorter man who was a little older than me, who told me to call him Bob. Tom then introduced me to the rest of the Group. There were sixteen of us altogether, a mixed group of strangers to me. However, most knew each other through bird watching activities. Russell came over to have a chat, and to introduce himself. He asked me to call him Rusty, as this was the name his friends called him. I felt quite at ease with him, and believed we would get on well with each other.

As I was talking to Rusty, Mr and Mrs Tyne appeared, followed by two of the Ladies who were sisters, called Connie Connelly and Enid Edding. This was very nice, and I immediately felt welcome. I thought I would not remember all their names, but perhaps over the next few days I could gradually remember some of them. We seemed to be around a similar age, mid to late forties, although one or two were perhaps a little older. We chatted for a while, trying to get to know one another, until it was time to go through Customs, and board the aircraft. We all indicated that we were looking forward to the trip, and seeing the birds and animals in their natural settings.

I found out that Mark Tyne was a Joiner by trade. He was tall, but not as tall as Tom. He seemed a little shy, but told me he loved photography. Maureen, his wife, was a College Domestic. She was tall and slim, with short dyed hair, and was more outgoing than Mark. Connie was a little older, and a former librarian. She was short, and appeared quite bubbly. Her sister, Enid, seemed slightly older and much slimmer. She told me she was a retired Sports Teacher, and still loved tennis. We talked about my experiences with tennis at school, instead of playing football. All of these were part of a birdwatching group, and the sisters in particular loved to travel.

The aircraft we boarded was a Jumbo Jet, for the journey which took us from Heathrow, via Frankfurt in Germany, to Egypt and down the Nile Valley, over The Sudan and Eritrea, to Addis Ababa in Ethiopia. There we were delayed approximately two and a half hours, waiting for our smaller aeroplane to arrive and take us to Kilimanjaro Airport. Whilst we were waiting, and as we were allowed, I went out of the airport in Addis, across to a local park to have a look around.

The whole area was thronged with local people, including many Soldiers armed with rifles. They looked at me curiously but did not bother me. Even so, once I had seen the tall buildings of Addis Ababa in the distance, I did not hang about but went back to find the others in the airport lounge. I could not find the male bird watchers at first, so I asked the ladies where they were. They pointed me in the direction of the gentlemen's toilets, which I thought was unusual in that they had all gone together. However, there they were, with the window wide open, watching a flock of interesting birds! They told me they were a species of Ibis endemic to Ethiopia, and it was the only place from which they could see them. At that point I realized that the group members were "true bird-watching enthusiasts".

We eventually took off in the smaller aircraft for Kilimanjaro airport, landing late in the afternoon, having circumvented the snow-covered Mount Kilimanjaro. I already knew that Kilimanjaro was a large extinct volcano, but to witness the crater, filled with snow, was impressive. Once we had landed and cleared Passport Control and Customs, we were greeted by our contact, Steve. He introduced us to our Drivers and Guides for the tour. They were called George, Hussain, Mustafa and Henry. They took us to the land rovers for our journey to Marangu Lodge. It had started to drizzle a little but it was quite warm, and they told us the journey would take about one and a half hours.

We put our bags and cases on racks on top of the land rovers, and set off for our accommodation for the night. The journey was quite long and it rained most of the way, but it was fairly clear by the time we arrived at the Lodge. I unpacked my large, light blue holdall, only to find it was not waterproof. I had to dry everything before bedtime. After being given time to settle in, we had an evening meal of tender beef and vegetables, including potatoes, carrots and parsnips. This was very tasty. I had a glass of lager to wash it down. The atmosphere was quite exciting and jovial, as we were all looking forward to visiting our first Wildlife Park the next day.

I had an opportunity to chat to Sidney Larkin, who introduced himself as Sid. He was a tall, solid built man, with messy looking hair and staring eyes. He told me he was a Music Teacher, with particular interests in Classical Music and Anthropology. He was looking forward to visiting the Olduvai Gorge, the site of Human Evolution and the birth of Homo Habilis. I found my chat with him quite interesting. His wife, Stephanie, a former Model, came over to join us at the Lodge bar. She was very tall and slim, with fashionable dark, curly hair. We all chatted for a while before returning to our rooms.

Looking at the map, our journey was going to take us from the Kilimanjaro region to Arusha National Park, Ngorongoro Crater, Serengeti, Lake Manyara and Tarangire, with stops along the way.

My Story now begins …

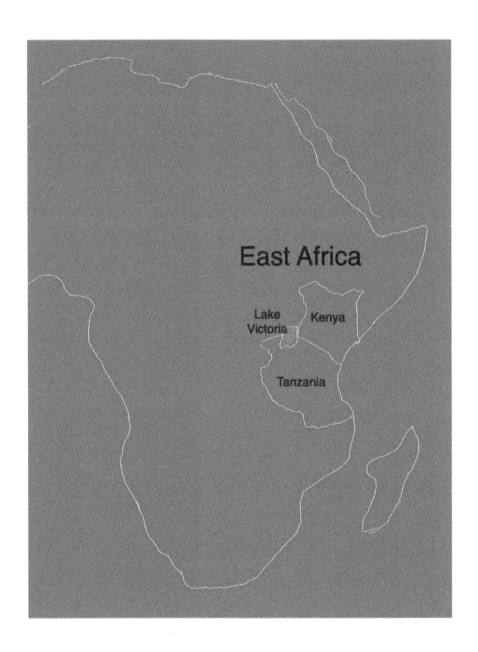

East Africa

Lake
Victoria

Kenya

Tanzania

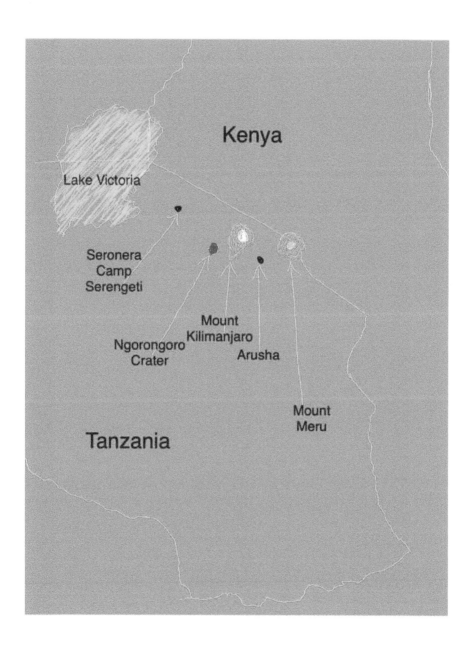

Kenya

Lake Victoria

Seronera
Camp
Serengeti

Mount
Kilimanjaro
Ngorongoro
Crater   Arusha

Mount
Meru

Tanzania

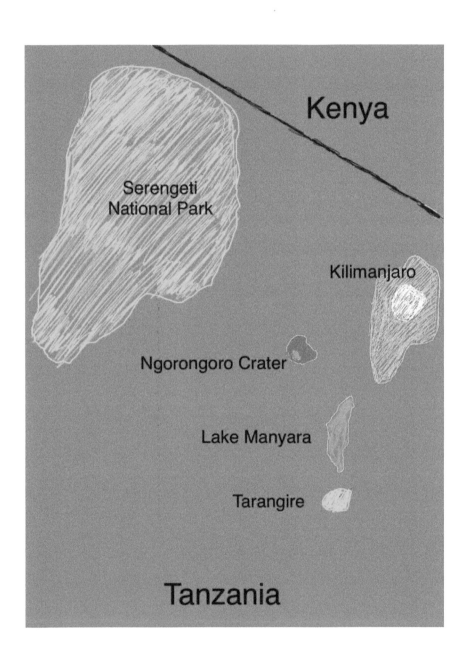

Chapter 1

First Impressions

It was a bright Sunday morning as I went for breakfast. I had had a poor night's sleep because of an ingrown eyelash. I had tried to wash it out in the night with a cup of water, after I had cleaned the ants off the cup. Eventually I pulled the eyelash out with my fingers in desperation. I hoped this was not an omen for my tour, because I had had to go to bed in the same shirt that I had been wearing all day, and I was also having to wear some of my clothes which were still damp. As the day was quite warm, I was hoping they would dry fairly quickly, even though they were rather creased. Not a good start or impression!!

The breakfast consisted of a kind of maize porridge, a local speciality which I barely tasted before rejecting. I opted for the scrambled egg on toast instead. This was something I would not normally have had. I mentioned to the others about my eye problem, as my eye was quite red and angry. Bob, Tom's friend, gave me some soothing eye drops, in the hope they would ease it. I thanked him for this, fearing it would spoil my trip if I didn't sort it out. Following breakfast, we had a tour around the subtropical gardens looking for bird species.

We admired the beautiful shrubs and plants, before gathering our things together, and leaving the Lodge to head off to explore the local area. We travelled with four people to each land rover, so Rusty and I shared with Mark and Maureen Tyne. Our driver was called Hussain.

The convoy set off towards the Tanzanian/Kenyan Border to visit Kilimanjaro National Park. This was set in the foothills of Mount Kilimanjaro. In that area we were looking for various bird species. The first group of birds I saw were Weaver Birds, little birds like our finches, fluttering around their nests which were made out of balls of grass and twigs, and were hanging from Acacia trees like baubles on a Christmas tree.

Figure 1 Weaver Bird

It was fascinating to watch them, as I had never seen them before. You would think that it only needed a gust of wind to blow the nests off the trees, but on closer inspection you could see they were well constructed. They were quite noisy birds, as if they were arguing with each other all the time. It was quite warm, so I had to adjust to the temperature, as it was fairly cold at home. At least my clothes had now dried!

After exploring the local area, we stopped for a picnic lunch. We had arrived on the rim of a water-filled Crater, which had formed a bright blue lake, called Lake Chala. This lake straddled the Kenyan Border. The Crater was surrounded by high walls of dense forest. From there we had excellent panoramic views across the Kenyan landscape.

The weather was very hot by that time, as we stood watching African Fish Eagles diving down towards the water hundreds of feet below us. The scene was very picturesque and, fortunately, we were high enough above the lake to see it. The keen birdwatching members had set up their scopes, and were pointing out and explaining the birds to us, such as the Fish Eagles and Tawny Eagles. I had gone over to have a look through the scopes, even though I had my binoculars with me, which I had bought twenty years previously. They were only low magnification compared to the scopes. The scopes were ideal for highlighting the birds' defining features.

Figure 2 African Fish Eagle

Our picnic lunch consisted of various cheese and meat sandwiches, with fizzy drinks and water to wash them down, followed by bananas and oranges. The trip so far had made a very good first impression, with wonderful scenery, bird sightings and a lovely picnic. We headed back towards the Lodge, exploring the area along the way.

The next day I got up early to have another wander around the garden, and to look at the colourful flowers. I particularly wanted to see the rustic Gazebo, covered in flowering shrubs, which I had briefly seen the day before. The garden was a colourful contrast to the bright blue sky, which was highlighting the snow-covered peaks of Kilimanjaro and Mount Meru.

We were heading off to our next park, where we were going to stay the night. This was called the Mkomazi Game Reserve.

On the way, the terrain was hilly and quite barren, almost like scrubland. I noticed that, as we passed through the Reserve to get to our accommodation, there were lots of large termite mounds, nearly as high as myself.

As we stopped to photograph them, I stared down at my feet, and at the reddish-brown soil. I caught sight of the large dung beetles rolling elephant dung, twice as big as themselves, along the ground. They were fascinating to watch.

Figure 3 Dung Beetle

As we drove further through the park, it was obvious that there were not as many animals around as expected. The Reserve was, however, better known for its birdlife, in which the Group was interested.

Further along the track, I did count sixteen giraffe in one herd, and I could see others on the horizon. I also saw many species of birds, from Herons and small birds such as Whydah birds, to some Birds of Prey. There were some highly coloured birds with which I was unfamiliar, not being a regular birdwatcher at that time. Even though I was not a regular birdwatcher like the others, their enthusiasm was infectious, and I was learning about new bird species all the time.

We arrived at the campsite, set on a rocky hillside, where we were given an option of accommodation. Rusty and I chose the traditional African Banda rather than a tent. It was a circular mud hut, with a thatched roof. I was looking forward to the experience of sleeping in one, and so was Rusty. In any case, I had experienced life in a tent back home, and with the Army, so that was an obvious choice for me on that occasion.

After settling into the accommodation, we all got together in the Mess Hut for an evening meal. As it was fairly light, some of the birdwatching members of the Group set up their scopes, to look out through the open walls of the hut. I decided to nip to the washroom Banda, to wash my hands etcetera, and was confronted by an unusual looking Wasp, over an inch long, on the window.

Figure 4 African Paper Wasp

I did not hang about, and managed to circle around it and get out quickly. Getting stung would not have been a good way to start the trip!!

We all sat at a long table in the Mess Hut, with oil lamps down the middle. I sat near the end, next to one of the lamps. It was getting darker as we started our meal, the first course being soup. I was beginning to realize that being in the jungle meant lots of insects, and this was no exception. Thousands were flying into the hut, striking the ceiling and falling down onto our table. I was trying to cover up my soup with my hand, only to find a large Beetle, the size of my spoon, bouncing off it. Everybody was laughing because the Host said, "we had another group of tourists here for a meal, and they said that the croutons were quite interesting. I didn't have the heart to tell them".

I carried on with my meal and covering it the best I could, while watching a small Praying Mantis, which had settled on the lamp in front of me, snatching at Gnats as they flew by.

Figure 5 Praying Mantis

I found all this fascinating. It was an enjoyable evening, and a good way to meet everybody. We were having fun, but I was very tired and looking forward to my bed.

Chapter 2

Onward To Explore Arusha National Park

Following a comfortable night in the Banda, we left the camp on the hillside shortly after breakfast, to investigate the wildlife in the Reserve once again. As I looked back at the camp the sky was quite cloudy, making the camp look eerie against the hills behind.

Figure 6 Hartebeest

We hadn't gone very far, and I could see Zebra, Hartebeest and Eland.
Passing through the Park Gate we were confronted by a group of Black-faced Vervet Monkeys, who were blocking the path of our land rovers. They eventually moved away, and we continued to explore the Reserve.

After exploring the Reserve for a while, we moved on to the Arusha National Park via Moshi, where we paused to fill up with petrol.

Here we were met by some of the local children selling oranges. "Oranges, oranges" they cried, as they crowded around our vehicles. One of the sisters, Enid, got out of the land rover to give them some sweets. The children were quite excited to see us.

As we drove along the road to Arusha, we passed a field full of Stork, with many more flying overhead. The roads in this part of the country were quite an experience. To describe them, and in particular the main road we were on, I would say they were "rough". There was a piece of tarmac in the middle, with loose stony edges and numerous deep potholes. As we made our way along the road, the land rovers were bouncing and jostling about, throwing up clouds of dust and debris. Because of the potholes, the drivers tended to seek out the smoother edges of the road, consequently creating mini whirlwinds of dust along the way. In addition to this, I could see several "dust devils" coming across the front of us, being created by the wind.

On the way to the Arusha National Park, our convoy halted at a very large crater rim, called The Ngurdoto Crater. I could see a large herd of African Buffalo on the Crater bottom. They were so far below from where I was standing that they looked like ants. This large, extinct volcanic Crater had walls covered in thick forest, which sloped down to the Crater's soggy bottom. I could see, through my binoculars, that it was lush, green and swampy. Standing there was not a place to be if you didn't have a head for heights!!

Arriving at the Arusha National Park, a highly wooded area on the slopes of Mount Meru, we paused for a rest and a drink, as the weather was becoming quite hot and humid.

Figure 7 Columbus Monkey

Some of us took a short walk along the track, to see the Columbus Monkeys. These were playing in the trees near the track, and I could see the black and white colouring of them, as they leapt about noisily once they were aware of our presence.

The first lake we planned to visit was Lake Logil.

It was about five o'clock in the afternoon as we stood on the bank of the lake, looking across to the other side at the Hippos and Birds. To our surprise, a herd of Elephants came out of the trees to drink at the water's edge. I counted twenty-five, twenty-six, twenty-seven, and they were still coming. Whole families of them. I just stood, looking at them through my binos in amazement. After a while they disappeared back into the trees, probably unaware that we were watching them. My attention moved to a number of Hippos, bobbing up and down in the water, over to my right. We discussed how dangerous these animals were, and agreed it was better to avoid them if possible.

Our next port of call was a big lake called Momella Lake.

Here I could saw lots of Buffalo, laid on the bank at the side of the lake. Others were making their way towards them, where I could see a flock of Egyptian Geese standing nearby. In the middle of the lake were several Pelicans.

Figure 8 Hippopotamus

Also, there was a Hippo with its head sticking out of the water. Its mouth was wide open, showing its enormous tusks.

I recognised a Spoonbill wading down to my left, behind a Water Buck, as you could not miss its distinctive beak. A Bushbuck stood not far away from him, at the front of the lake. I didn't know where to look next, as people were shouting and pointing in all directions. The excitement was quite infectious.

We observed the lake's wildlife for about a quarter of an hour, before moving on our way again. Banded Mongooses were moving across the track in front of us. This caused some excitement in our land rover. A large Waterbuck, with long horns, greeted us at the next lake we visited.

Figure 9 Dik Dik

I could just see a well camouflaged Dik Dik in the long grass, and tried to photograph it. It was quite a cute, small antelope.

Everyone was getting excited at the sight of a Red-billed Saddle Stork, which we could clearly see walking towards us through some Sacred Ibis and Egrets. Another Stork could be seen flying across the lake, as we left to go back to a local Lodge for refreshments. The refreshments were welcome as it had been quite hot in this area. I spent a little time with Mark and Maureen that day. Mark had a small video camera with him. I wished I had one, or a better camera. Rusty had a nice camera, and told me he was very selective about which photographs he took, while I just snapped away.

It was now after six, and the light was beginning to fade as we passed a group of Giraffe. Unfortunately, it had begun to rain and we were getting wet, so our driver, George, stopped to put the land rover canopy up before proceeding to our hotel for the night. Soon it was pouring down, making the rough bumpy track turn into a stream, and then a river. Twenty minutes after leaving the lakeside, the rain was really heavy, but I could still see a Dik Dik running across the track, splashing through the muddy river in front of us. Leaving the Park boundary, we could just make out a herd of about forty Buffalo, a hundred yards to our left.

We arrived in Arusha in the evening, to stay at the Impala hotel in the middle of town. It was a four-storey concrete building, with balconies at the front. Most of us sat in the outside bar area, chatting and having a drink, before going to our rooms. I sat with two friends, Daphne Pitman, a School Secretary, and Ivy Winston-Holme, a School Cook. I had not had much contact with them before. Both Ladies appeared to be a little older than me. Daphne was short and slender, with plain long grey hair. I found her quite approachable and a friendly, attentive woman. Ivy was slightly shorter than Daphne, with short curly hair. Ivy bought me a drink and asked me to join them. We sat also with Mark and Maureen, the couple with whom I had spent most of the day, as well as with Rusty. We felt hungry and discussed the meal ahead, as well as the day's events, before going to our rooms to get ready for the evening meal. I thought the ladies felt quite sorry for me because of my very creased outfit. It was now eight o'clock and I was showered and ready for the meal. I found the hotel quite comfortable, with all the mod cons required.

Back in the bedroom, after the enjoyable evening meal, and looking out of the window I could see in the darkness, through the car headlights, people walking about and a group of teenagers sitting in the road. Before retiring for the night, Rusty and I reflected again on the day's events. We felt we had had a marvellous day, and it seemed like weeks since we had started this adventure.

Chapter 3

The Road to Gibb's Farm and the Great Rift Valley

After a lie-in and breakfast, we left the Impala Hotel in Arusha, and headed for Gibb's Farm where we were to stay for lunch. Our journey took us along the new Italian-constructed highway, out of Arusha towards Lake Manyara, at the foot of the Rift Valley.

Driving through open country, with a few shrubs scattered here and there, we passed Maasai settlements. These were characterized by their mud and straw Bandas, surrounded by a stockade type boundary.

From time-to-time we passed Maasai, tending their small herds of cattle. Occasionally we could see various species of birds, soaring overhead.

Figure 10 Abdim's Stork

We passed under many magnificent Abdim's Stork, spiralling upwards on the thermals, with their black wings catching the eye as the sun glistened against their whitish bodies.

It was just past midday when we began to climb higher towards our destination, the Farm where we were looking forward to the magnificent feast, about which we had been told. The terrain was beginning to change from the wide-open scrubland to more bushy areas, with thorn bushes lining the roadsides. A Kite flew by, with its white front and head, and black wings, immediately recognisable to the knowledgeable, but not to me, although I was pleased with myself for recognising it as a Kite. The roadsides were now scattered more numerously with the small Maasai settlements, only here the bandas were surrounded by thorn bush fences, reflecting the type of terrain.

At a crossroads along the way, we paused for a while so that a puncture could be temporarily repaired on one of the land rovers.

We were immediately surrounded by a group of Maasai women, chatting and giggling whilst they attempted to display their handicrafts to us. The bangles, necklaces and other decorations were made from tiny coloured beads, and were quite pretty. The Maasai women, dressed in their red outfits and shawls, were babbling on excitedly, but no-one could understand a word they were saying, including the drivers. Apparently the Maasai language, which is centuries old, is quite unique. A couple of the women from our group bought some of the jewellery, whilst the puncture was being repaired, and we then moved on to our next destination.

The road was to take us out of the town, past Lake Manyara in the distance, and up into the hills. Unfortunately, after just leaving the town, we came upon a troop of Baboons, and one of them had been knocked down in the road and killed just before we arrived. A sad sight, and one that reflected the expanding commercialization of the area, and the difficulties of man and his technology living in harmony with nature and its wildlife. The local people had gently moved the dead Baboon to one side of the road, so that we could drive on.

The road was steep, but the land rovers made short work of it. At the top of the Rift Valley, we paused to admire the view. We were told that the Great Rift Valley was about three thousand miles in length, and was believed to have been formed by the sinking and tearing apart of the Earth's crust, along a fifty-million-year-old fault. We were also told that it varies in height from nearly fifteen hundred feet below sea level, at the shore of the Dead Sea in Jordan, to six thousand feet above sea level at cliffs in Kenya.

Lake Manyara

Lake Manyara lies at the foot of the Rift Valley surrounded by high cliffs, and stretches as far as the eye can see.

As we looked out over the top of the cliff, an amazing sight enveloped us. Besides the thousands and thousands of Flamingos and Pelicans, spiralling up on the thermals from the lake surface, there were even more on the edge of the lake. "What an amazing feast for the eye to behold", I thought, "maybe only once seen but never forgotten". Bob estimated there to be at least three quarters of a million Flamingos on the lake's edges.

It would be impossible to reproduce such a sight in a photograph, or even on video. It would be difficult to experience that same feeling, other than to actually be standing there on that cliff, looking out over the lake. It was truly a stunning sight, out of this world, or at least a sight rarely witnessed elsewhere in the World. I felt in awe, as I stood looking in amazement at what was before me.

Along with the Pelicans and Flamingos flying over the lake, I could see Eagles and Vultures soaring in amongst them. Down to my left there were many of the wild animals which roam the banks of the lake. Giraffe, Wildebeest, Buffalo and Elephant in abundance, but it was time to press on to Gibb's Farm for lunch. We would visit the lake again later in the week.

On reaching Gibb's Farm, we were seated in groups in the garden around small wooden tables, overlooking the valley below. We were surrounded by exotic tropical plants and brightly coloured flowers. The sun was beaming down, creating a most beautiful setting, and we were replenishing our appetites on the various cold meats, such as chicken, ham and beef. Exotic fruits and freshly baked bread were also laid out in front of us.

As expected, the buffet lunch was excellent, with plenty of food for everyone. No-one was disappointed, and everyone tucked into the feast accordingly.

After adequately replenishing ourselves with lunch, one group settled down to relax in the warm sunshine, whilst another smaller group, including myself, decided to go up into the nearby forest to see what we could find. Besides, I was frightened of missing something, being a curious person. We came across a number of brightly coloured Bee-eaters, including a Cinnamon-breasted Bee-eater, with its green back and yellow pointed beak distinguishing it from the thick green foliage.

Figure 11 Black-headed Oriole

The sighting of a Black-Headed Oriole created some excitement, as we headed back to the Farm to meet up with the rest of the party.

From the Farm we moved onto the rim of the area's largest volcanic crater, the Ngorongoro Crater.

Chapter 4

Into the Ngorongoro Crater

At the Ngorongoro Crater rim

The Ngorongoro Crater is the World's largest extinct volcanic crater, some ten miles across. We stopped on the Crater rim to pose for photographs, near the Crater Rim Lodge, before we descended the two thousand feet into the crater bottom. From there I could see the wall at the other side of the Crater, covered in thick forest, and the large lake in the middle.

Hussain, our Driver, told us that the Crater was one of the most incredible wild animal sanctuaries in Africa, without exaggeration. We expected to see some of the four large prides of Lions that live there, along with other predators. This would be our first sighting of lions, and we were all very excited at the prospect. Up to that point we had not really seen any predators.

Hussain drove us down a very steep, very stony, very narrow and very bumpy track, and we were all hanging on for dear life! Rusty and I were sharing the land rover with Daphne and Ivy, with whom we had been chatting at the hotel the day before. The ladies felt nervous, and were avoiding looking at the sheer drop on one side of the track, as Hussain skilfully drove us down to the Crater bottom. Nevertheless, the resulting journey's end was more than worthy of the hardship.

As we moved across the Crater bottom, Hussain pointed out Lake Magadi as the largest lake in the Crater. I saw lots of Flamingos around the Lake, and a feast of wild animals. These included herds of Zebra, Wildebeest, Buffalo and Antelope as far as the eye could see. The plethora of animals continued until we reached our tented camp, on the opposite side of the crater from which we had entered. This tented camp was to be our home for the next two nights. I thought to myself, "mm... amongst the wildlife, sleeping in a tent, my goodness, with only canvas between those ferocious beasts and me!". "What about the lions?" I said, but no-one replied. They were just standing, staring at our accommodation. "I am sure that I am tastier than a Wildebeest", I remarked. We were met by our host who told us not to worry as no-one had ever been pulled from their tent, well up to then anyway. This was reassuring at least.

We were shown to our grey two-man tents, which had camp beds. There was a canvas bowl outside for washing. Time had been given for us to settle in, before being asked to report to the Mess Tent for an evening meal.

As it had been a long day travelling, everyone decided to retire early for the night but, before settling down, Rusty and I tried to clear the insects out of the tent.

Ngorongoro Crater camp kitchen

I survived the first night and, surprisingly, slept well. Probably my snoring kept all the wild animals away! It certainly kept Rusty awake. After a few apologies to him and a hearty breakfast, prepared for us in the camp kitchen, we set off in our land rovers in search of more animals and birds. The first thing to hit my senses that morning was the thick mist over the lake. There were cotton wool clouds on top of the rim surrounding the crater, and covering the thick forest.

We were not long out of the camp, on this bright Thursday morning, before we saw Zebra and Wildebeest grazing on the short green grasslands.

I remarked, "a real Zebra crossing", but it went down like a lead balloon.
The abundance of wildlife was breath-taking. Everywhere I looked there were, literally, thousands of animals and birds.

Black-backed Jackal

As we drove along the track, we surprised a Black-backed Jackal heading in our direction, but it changed its mind as we approached.

Further on a pack of Hyenas were eating the head of a Wildebeest. I could even hear the crunching of the bones, as their powerful jaws closed in on the kill. The ladies, sharing our land rover, cringed at this. Vultures, waiting for their share of the spoils, surrounded these Hyenas.

One of the larger Vultures had its wings outstretched. It looked enormous from our distance of twenty-five yards. Maybe it was trying to scare off the Hyenas, but it had no chance. Hussain told us it was a Griffon Vulture, one of the largest in Africa.

Figure 12 Griffon Vulture

A few moments later, I was filled with excitement as I saw my first Lions! Suddenly before us were two young male Lions, which appeared to be stalking prey, but they didn't look too interested in catching it. Maybe we disturbed them.

A mother Wildebeest, with two young ones in tow, was being chased by another pack of Hyenas with serious intent on getting a tasty meal. As we made our way from the shorter grassy areas, towards the longer and lush grasslands, I saw a couple of Elephants grazing. They were unconcerned as the vehicles passed by. As we drew nearer to the longer grasslands of the Crater, our land rover developed a puncture. We all got out while Hussain changed the wheel. We were surrounded by animals staring at us, and we stared back at them. I bet they were thinking, "who are these curious creatures?"

In particular, three Wildebeest were staring intensely at me, only forty yards or so from where I was standing. I was standing rigid and apprehensive, but trying not to show it, and all passed off uneventfully.

Having had the wheel changed, we moved off once again towards the lush, greener and wooded areas of the crater floor. We had our first sighting of Ostriches, but they were too far off to be seen clearly without binoculars.

As we entered that area of the Crater, we suddenly came across a lone, and rather large, male Lion. He was lying on his left-hand side in the longer grass, soaking up the sun. He just lifted his head to look at us, before deciding to sink back into his totally relaxed and dreamy state, maybe dreaming of his next meal, but it was not going to be us!! He certainly seemed uninterested in people, and what we were about.

Still further into this grassier area, and completely by accident, we stumbled across a pride of Lions, feeding on a Zebra.

I could see a mother and small cub amongst them.

It was hard to watch the carnage of it, but it was the natural "law of the jungle". It didn't take away the great feeling of seeing number four on the list of the "great five". Without warning another of the younger Lions just picked up a striped leg and carried it off.

In that area I saw more Jackals, and some Grant's Gazelle over by a watering hole, where four large Elephants were standing, drinking. Our land rover approached one Elephant, which was standing in some long grass, eating.

It let us come within twenty yards of it, without appearing to be disturbed, as it continued its meal. Unfortunately for the photographers, it did not turn around to show its best side.

We arrived at the Crater's main Hippo pool, where I was able to get out of the land rover and go nearer to the water's edge, to take photos of the Hippos.

However, the Hippos had other ideas and remained submerged, with only their ears and nostrils sticking out of the water. Over to my right, I saw some partially submerged Hippos, but I was obstructed from enjoying a clear view of them by some long green reeds in that part of the pool. Looking up into the tree, under which I was standing by the Hippo pool, I could see a Black Kite which was peering down at me from its perch.

Figure 13 Hamerkop

Close to the Black Kite was a Hamerkop, standing at the water's edge. After a fairly lengthy time, taking in the serenity and beauty of the Hippo pool, we left and headed towards Black Rhino country.

Chapter 5

Black Rhino Country

As we drove on towards the Black Rhino country we were still surrounded by a host of animals. They included Zebra, Wildebeest, Grant's Gazelle and another Black-backed Jackal. By then we were beginning to draw closer to the Ostriches, grey coloured females. I could clearly see a mother and baby Ostrich to my left, but they scurried away as our land rovers closed in on them. "What fast movers" I thought to myself.

To me, approaching the Black Rhino was quite an emotional experience, as they are one of the world's most endangered species. They can live up to fifty years old.

I could see five huge creatures in front of me which was quite a sight, with the sun behind highlighting their magnificent silhouettes. They were not really black, but a dark dusty grey. As I stood in the land rover watching this group of Rhinos, another very large one, accompanied by a smaller one, came across behind the vehicle, totally ignoring it. It was difficult for us to ignore them.

As Hussain approached the two Rhino for us to get closer photos, we soon got their attention, and the larger of the two turned towards us. We were crouching on our seats by now, as Hussain swerved the land rover out of the path of the now pursuing Rhino, which had picked up speed as it tried to charge us. Our skilful driver was keeping his foot down on the accelerator, thereby keeping a safe margin between the land rover and the Rhino's long pointed horn. As we turned once more, the Rhino charged again, just missing the land rover's rear wheel where I was sitting. I gave a groan, but the sheer driving skill of Hussain ensured that I would be in no danger. In any case, I didn't fancy one of those magnificent Rhino horns up my "rear suspension!".

The Rhino gave up and moved off to join the others. I scraped myself off the seat and, in a show of relief with Rusty, Daphne and Ivy who were sharing my land rover that day, applauded Hussain for demonstrating his skill. Of course, I knew I was in no danger from the Rhino or, at least, I reassured myself that I was not. It seemed much longer than it was, but we stayed to observe these magnificent animals for twenty minutes or so, gazing in awe at their sheer size and presence.

Figure 14 Red-billed Oxpecker

I could see that one of the three Rhinos, standing in front of the land rover, had a Red-billed Oxpecker on its back.

Over to my right, about twenty yards away, were a couple of African Crowned Cranes, and behind them stood a small group of Thompson's Gazelle, grazing.

Figure 15 African Crowned Crane

Moving back to the camp we passed some more Crowned Cranes, but they did not hang around as the land rovers approached them. I observed even more herds of Zebra and Hartebeest. It was eleven o'clock as we came in sight of the camp, and passed the Rangers on patrol. The weather was cloudier, and I noticed that the air smelled like a farmyard. I thought, "this is what you don't experience from the television programmes". Another thing about the country was the sheer number of insects about, everywhere we went.

The tented camp itself stood by a row of trees and was surrounded by thousands of animals. Behind the camp flowed a small river and, on the hilly areas of the Crater, were herds of Buffalo. In front, and either side of the camp were herds of Zebra, Wildebeest and Antelope, with Lions, Hyena and other scavengers roaming about. The previous night in the camp I had heard a Lion roar, but generally I was surprised by how quiet it was. I had expected it to be very noisy with all these animals about.

It was twenty to one in the afternoon. Other members of the group were doing their own thing, writing a diary or reading. Some had gone down to a nearby lake to see the Flamingos. I had washed my "smalls" in the makeshift canvas camp sink, outside the tent, using the brown coloured water from the river nearby. The water had done its job, and they were soon hanging in the sun to dry. As I looked out from the mess tent, I could see a group of Wildebeest, about a thousand yards away, looking in. Either side of us were Zebra and Gazelle, having their lunch.

Chapter 6

Visiting the Hills, Lakes and Woods of the Crater

After lunch we set off again towards the hillier areas behind the camp and, therefore, towards the Buffalo I had spotted in the distance earlier.

Figure 16 African Buffalo

It was a large herd of Buffalo which, as we drew near, I could see through my binoculars were covered in Cattle Egrets.

Figure 17 Cattle Egret

There must have been some two hundred African Buffalo spread over both sides of the hill, to the right of my vehicle. There were flocks of Egrets flying over the Buffalo as we got a little closer to them.

A small herd of Elephants had appeared to our right, as we moved briskly along the track. We nearly ran into two Black-backed Jackals which came from literally nowhere, and were going across the track in front of our lead land rover.

The Crater had various areas where the animals lived. It appeared to be divided into the short grass grazing areas, the longer grasslands, the wooded areas, and the hilly parts where we were visiting the large herds of Buffalo.

In addition, there was the large Lake Magadi in the centre, where the Flamingos and other wading and water birds lived. Up to the rim of the Crater, some two thousand feet high, were extensive rain forests.

We entered the longer grasslands again, but in a different part of the Crater to that visited that morning.

An African Marsh Harrier was circling overhead, when suddenly a Hyena popped its head up above the long grass. "You would not have known it was there", I thought. "It is quite a ferocious animal, the Hyena, very scary. Its bite can be a thousand pounds of force, and it can eat a third of its weight in one meal. I certainly wouldn't want to cuddle one!"

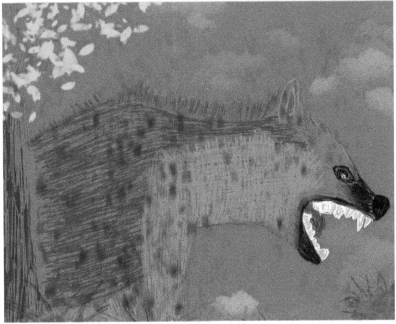

Figure 18 Spotted Hyena

52

More Crowned Cranes appeared as we moved towards the lakeside. On the smaller pools by the lake, I could see Flamingos and Sacred Ibis in abundance, wading and feeding peacefully in the afternoon sunlight.

The time was coming up to four in the afternoon, as we continued to make our way along the shore of the lake. This was illuminated with the "flaming" sight of Flamingos.

Near some reeds, I saw a couple of Kori Bustards being stalked by a Golden Jackal, only twenty yards from the land rover.

Figure 19 Kori Bustard

53

For some inexplicable reason the Jackal stopped and started to dig. A Marsh Harrier flew overhead, as some Grant's Gazelle grazed behind the Jackal. A group of four or five Warthogs peered out from a dip, beyond the Gazelle. I wondered if this was their den.

After pausing for a while to watch, we moved on towards the main area of the lake, where I could see hundreds and hundreds of Lesser Flamingo, wading in the soda water. In front of them was a flock of Chestnut-banded Plover. Over to the right, in another small pool, were Glossy Ibis, Grey-headed Gulls, Black-winged Stilts and a whole variety of Ducks and Geese. Still more varieties of birds adorned the pools, Black-winged and Spur-winged Plover were easily identifiable. Further on, the second land rover nearly ran over a Hamerkop, with its dull russet brown plumage contrasting well with the soil on the track. However, the bird wisely took off first. As we turned right a couple of Crowned Cranes were displaying. A Yellow Wagtail stood in front of a herd of Thompson's Gazelle, which were peacefully grazing. My senses were being constantly bombarded by the wealth of wildlife around me.

We left the lakeside, and found a pride of twelve Lions basking in the hot sun, even though it was getting late into the afternoon.

These Lions were not "batting an eyelid", as we stopped for the obligatory photographs. Hussain told us that Lions were opportunist hunters during the night or day and when they were not hunting, they slept a great deal.

Further on we came across a group of Bat-eared Foxes, but they were rather timid and ran away from us. The habitat was by now quite lush and very green, with more pools of muddy water and shrubs around.

Here we ventured close to a small herd of twenty Buffalo, laid in the mud by the water's edge. Some were covered in mud to keep them cool, which gave them an eerie, light grey appearance to their already awesome bodies. The Buffalo is not an animal with which to tangle, as they can be very dangerous when cornered. The mud made them look even more ferocious.

Entering the wooded areas, nearer the Crater walls, I saw a large herd of Elephants moving through the trees some distance away. This herd consisted of females and their offspring. The large bull Elephants tended to wander off, and had been known to stray miles away from the herd. We decided to go looking for one, and found one standing in a pool of water, feeding. It was a glorious sight, and notably he still had his enormous tusks intact. So big were his tusks that they nearly touched the ground, and each other. Through Hussain's skill once again, he was able to creep close to the bull Elephant so we could take photographs.

In a large clearing, close to the wooded area and near another pool, we came across some Waterbuck and a large troop of around a hundred Baboons, wanting to cross the track in front of our land rovers.

The Waterbuck moved back over to the poolside, but the Baboons were determined to go into the trees across the track. They were screeching and playing "merry hell" because the vehicles were in their way. Two of the large males were chasing the little ones across the path, making them shriek in a high-pitched scream. We gave way to them by moving further into the trees. The Baboons then went about their business, albeit noisily.

In the bow of a tree, where our land rover stood, there was a Black-faced Monkey sitting and holding the tiniest baby I had ever seen. Deeper into the wooded area and amongst the trees, but still clearly visible to me, were more Elephants. Some of them had large tusks, highlighting the level of protection from poachers these animals were awarded. On a tall, fairly bare tree, at the edge of the wooded area I saw a flock of enormous sinister looking Marabou Stork. I thought that they were the ugliest birds I had ever seen, and they made me cringe even from that distance. While looking at these Marabou Stork, perched like silhouetted statues on the tree against the evening sunlight, I heard a Woodpecker hammering away nearby. No matter how hard I looked through my binoculars I could not, for the life of me, see the darned thing, until we moved around the tree where it was hammering. "At last," I sighed, as I got sight of the Grey Woodpecker. As we moved out from the trees, a White-browed Coucal came into view. Its head and chest looked fairly grey to me, with a horizontal black stripe from its beak and across its eye, with reddish-brown wings.

From the wooded area we travelled along the far side of the large lake, heading back towards the camp area. Along the shore, close to some reed beds, we saw a small group of four Elephants standing by the water's edge, with another two laid down on the side. As we passed these at a reasonable distance, and headed nearer towards the shore of the lake, near the reeds a Black-backed Jackal suddenly appeared with a goose in its mouth, and began to run away. This was being closely pursued by a Golden Jackal, which caught up with the Black-backed Jackal, and snatched the goose from it. We stood back and just watched in amazement, because our attention had been momentarily diverted from watching a couple of Fish Eagles, in a nearby tree. Another Black-backed Jackal had appeared, with a goose wing in its mouth, and the Golden Jackal had spotted it, and had begun to head towards it. This had caused the Black-backed Jackal to drop the wing and run off with its mate. I saw that the Golden Jackal seemed about the same size as the Black-backed Jackal, but was obviously the more aggressive of the two. Consequently, it had won all the spoils of the hunt. In all this excitement a little Dik Dik stood and watched from the side lines.

It was six-thirty in the evening as we headed back towards the camp, just as the sun was sinking over the rim of the crater. We were met by the Wardens, who told us that we should have been back in camp by that time. The Wardens, who were armed "to the teeth", were patrolling, and keeping an eye on two Black Rhino which had strayed near to the side of the track.

The Wardens explained to us that they had had a problem with poachers and, in nineteen eighty-seven, two of these valuable creatures were killed near to where we were. We were roughly in the central area of the Crater. The Wardens were, therefore, keen to enforce the curfew within the Crater, and were emphasizing this to the Drivers, who made profound apologies, and assurances that this would not happen again. We were allowed to move onward to the camp.

Chapter 7

An Eventful Night in Camp

The five-mile journey back into the camp, from where we met the Wardens, took us through various habitats. As we drove along, and as the light faded, we saw Elephants, Buffalo, Hyena, hundreds of birds and thousands of Zebra, Wildebeest and Antelope. It was fairly dark as we entered the tented area.

Sitting around the campfire, after our evening meal, we reflected on the fact that the Crater itself was a marvellous place, with some hundred and twelve square miles of grasslands, wooded areas and wetlands. Each area supported animals which breed and feed there. I saw a fair selection of these areas in the first couple of days there. The marvellous thing about it was, that one could not go more than a few yards without seeing a different species of animal, bird or insect. On the short grasslands we saw Zebra and Wildebeest, residing with their scavengers, the Lions, Hyena and Jackals. The longer and wetter grasslands provided food for the Rhino, Elephant and Buffalo. The wooded areas supported Monkeys, Baboons and a host of birds, whilst the Wetlands and Lakes supported Hippos and water birds. In addition to these areas, the sides of the Crater, reaching some two thousand feet high, were adorned with rain forests supporting yet more species of animals and birds, as well as those which strayed from the Crater floor. It had been a long, marvellous and very interesting day. However, it had been very hot, and I was tired and went to my bed.

I was awoken before dawn by something on the outside of the tent, pushing against my back. It made me jump because I had been dreaming. I turned over quickly to see its silhouette in the camp lights. It looked round like a snake, but I didn't know what type of snake it was. We had been warned there were green Mambas behind us near the river bed, and that they were large venomous snakes. It could not get into the tent but it still gave me a fright. I decided, after much deliberation, to get my torch and look outside, only to find that a tree branch had fallen against the tent, near my bed. "Some snake that was", I thought!!

I was shivering, not because of the snake incident, but because it was quite cold out of the tent. I returned to the tent and got back into my sleeping bag, snuggling up into it, trying to relax and go back to sleep, in order not to disturb Rusty.

Figure 20 African Green Mamba (Venomous)

I was just drifting back to sleep, when I was alerted by a sudden loud growling. It had even disturbed Rusty, who had jumped up out of bed. The Camp Staff were shouting around the camp. Someone had seen two Lions about one hundred yards from the camp, and near the corner of the hedgerow not far from where we were. Apparently, the Lions had walked out into the open area of the camp, before sloping off into the bush. I tried to get back to sleep again, but dawn quickly approached. I, therefore, decided to get up and go to the Mess Tent for a pot of tea.

The previous day, we had visited two of the four prides of Lions in the area of the Crater, and had seen lots more Elephants. Henry told me that there were some four hundred Lions altogether in the ten areas around the crater. To me, this seemed a very high number. However, if you considered the thousands of animals that they fed on, it was not.

We were having breakfast, and the group leader, Tom, told us that he saw four Lions by the camp earlier that morning, while he was using the facilities about one hundred feet from the tents. I wanted to use the facilities, but I was nervous as it was only a toilet tent. Henry advised that the new camp site was not good because the Lions came around into the camp at night, so they wanted to move the campsite, and not use it again for the tourists. He said they would move the camp away from the river, because the river flowing behind the camp attracted the elephants and other animals, and the Lions came hunting them. I said, "So now you tell us!"

We often had meetings to discuss the day's activities, or to reflect on the numbers of birds and animals sighted. These meetings, or rather get-togethers, occurred on an evening over a relaxing drink around the campfire, or were held round about meal times, when we were waiting to dine. The reflection that morning included the sighting from the previous afternoon, as we came back into camp. We could see what was thought to be smoke in the distance, over the hedgerow behind the camp. However, as we got closer, it turned out to be an extremely large flock of Egrets, flying up and down the hedgerow. Behind them, on the hillside at the back of the camp, were masses of Buffalo, lined up like eighteenth century soldiers waiting to go into battle. The Egrets flew off towards the forests around the two-thousand feet high crater wall, once the evening had drawn in. The larger trees around the camp were covered in Vultures and Stork.

Chapter 8

Out of the Crater

A beautiful day greeted me and, although I had a war going on in my insides, I was looking forward to the day's events with excitement.

Everyone was beginning to get their bags or cases together, and take them to the land rovers, because we were leaving the crater area and moving on to the vast plains of the Serengeti. Some of the bird watchers had set up a scope to look at a Peregrine Falcon in the tree by the camp. After putting my bag on the top of the land rover, I ventured over to look at the bird through the scope. I could see that we were surrounded, yet again, by thousands of animals.

We set off from the camp, and I could see another Falcon over to my left-hand side, and lots of Helmeted Guinea Fowl wandering about. One of the land rovers had developed a puncture. It was the seventh this week. The cause of this puncture was a small piece of metal, about half an inch in diameter, stuck in between the tread of the tyre. There seemed to be a problem with old nails and bits falling off vehicles on these rough tracks, as they bounced about on the very uneven surfaces, and stony areas. Once the tyre had been changed, we were off again, and passed the area where I had seen the Hyena eating the Wildebeest head. There were plenty of Hyena and Wildebeest there, but the scene was peaceful, with some of the hundreds and hundreds of Wildebeest actually lying down in the grass. There were lots of Abdim's Stork walking about. We were moving towards a small lake and wooded area of the crater side, through the longer grassland. I observed six Elephants over to my left, and five Rhinos to the right of the track. We kept our distance from them this time.

I saw, amongst the many Geese, a Great Crested Grebe.

Figure 21 Great-crested Grebe

This is one of my favourite water birds, which I like to see when Angling. I like the way they carry their young on their backs, and I have spent many a happy hour watching them while not catching any fish!

Three Buffalo walked across from the wooded area on the right, towards the lake on my left. Near a clump of reeds two male Lions appeared as if from nowhere, and stood drinking from the lake. In the blink of an eye, one of the Lions had disappeared back into the reeds as quickly as it had appeared. "It goes to show", I thought, "one minute it was so peaceful and, in such a beautiful setting, I could have popped out of the land rover, and walked quite innocently down to the side of the lake to look at the birds, totally unaware of the Lions lurking in the reeds". I was reminded that this was Africa, with danger lurking around every corner as it did in that case. A short distance from the reed bed, a group of Hippos stood half in and half out of the water, with Egrets perched on their backs.

Heading into the forest at the foot of the crater wall, and towards a different route out of the crater, we passed some large Elephants some distance away from us, in the trees. The land rovers bounced over rough ground, which gave the appearance of a dried up river bed. Volcanic boulders littered the track, as it wound its way up the very steep crater side to the rim. I held on "for dear life", as I felt that it was one of the roughest rides I had encountered so far, with the land rover bumping and bashing its way out of the crater. At times the track seemed only just wide enough for the land rover, with a sheer drop on one side. However, the deep ruts kept the vehicle in the track, as it moved upwards under Hussain's skill. We went up through the dense forest, where there were many varieties of trees, and onto the top of the crater wall. We came out of the crater, and headed for the Lodge on the rim. There we stopped for refreshments, which gave the drivers time to fix the punctures in the spare tyres, before we moved onto the Serengeti. It appeared that there were problems obtaining replacement tyres for the vehicles, so the drivers were constantly having to repair them.

I sat at a table on the lawn, in the front garden of the Lodge, drinking a cool beer with some of the others. I looked out over towards the lake in the centre of the crater hundreds of feet below me, and across to the other side where I had spent the past two nights in the river-side campsite. "What a spectacular panoramic view it is", I said. The others agreed with me, and began to talk about their experiences of life in the camp.

However, our conversation was interrupted by the Manager of the Lodge, who came out to warn us not to wander away from the immediate area of the garden, because Hyena and Buffalo had been seen near the top of the crater rim. The Manager was quite concerned when Maggie told him that Tom and Bob had gone off into the woods, searching for unusual bird species. Thankfully, they returned soon after to the relief of everyone. We told them what the Manager had said, and they looked very relieved that they were back.

With the group refreshed and the tyres repaired, the convoy moved off around the crater rim, to the track that was to take us down onto the Serengeti. We passed several Giraffe, feeding on the thick thorn bushes on top of the hill leading up to the crater rim. Descending from the hills we started to see Zebra and Grant's Gazelle. The road was rough, more like a track made with volcanic rubble that had been levelled off at some time.

Stretching out in front of us, as we continued down the hill, was a vast plain. It looked green at that time of year, with the fluffy white clouds reflecting on the ground as darker green patches. It was hot, with the sun beaming down out of the blue sky. As we sped on to our next destination, we were temporarily slowed by Zebra crossing in front of us. As I looked out across the plain at the Zebra moving away, one of the land rovers overtook us, kicking up a dense cloud of dust as it passed. The thorn bushes were becoming thicker and wider spread, as we moved further towards the plain. So thick, that it was becoming difficult to see the animals, as they were hidden in the dense undergrowth. The rolling hills and green lush undergrowth reminded me of the Glens of Scotland, with hot sunshine of course. The big difference was that in Scotland we could just stop and wander about at will, but that could be a problem here with the wild animals around.

We were nearing the entrance to the Serengeti, a vast plain stretching for hundreds of miles. To me it looked quite green, with the short grasslands strewn with yet more thorn bushes and Acacia trees, which offered the only shelter from the fierce sun. "It is so hot", I thought, as the intense heat enveloped my body. The thermometer showed thirty-two degrees Celsius, but it seemed hotter to me in the direct sunlight.

Looking behind me, towards the rim of the crater we had left behind, I could see thick rain clouds hugging the top of the ridge. "What a contrast", I thought, "it's probably raining there and it seems exceptionally hot here". I pulled my hat closer down over my eyes, and continued to observe the terrain around me. As we got closer to the Serengeti Plain, I noticed several animal skulls and bones around, particularly on the bare patches of ground that had not yet become green like the rest of the terrain.

At the entrance to the Serengeti we halted, so that the group had an opportunity to view the Olduvai Gorge and Visitors' Centre.

Chapter 9

The Olduvai Gorge and Human Evolution

We travelled about thirty-six miles from the Ngorongoro Crater Rim, on a very bumpy, roughly gravelled track, to the eastern boundary of the Serengeti, and a small Visitors' Centre near the edge of the Olduvai Gorge. On arrival we enjoyed some refreshments, and the Centre Guide gave us a talk on the Gorge and of its findings. He also showed us some of the fossils and artefacts found in the gorge, and where they had been found. I sat on a window ledge and listened intently to the Speaker, whose name was Joe.

Joe told us that Human Evolution was a branch of Physical Anthropology.

This was widely known because of the work of a family of British

Paleoanthropologists, called Louis Leakey, his wife Mary and their son Richard. Their discovery of a series of fossils, in the Olduvai Gorge, had led to major revisions in the understanding of human biological evolution.

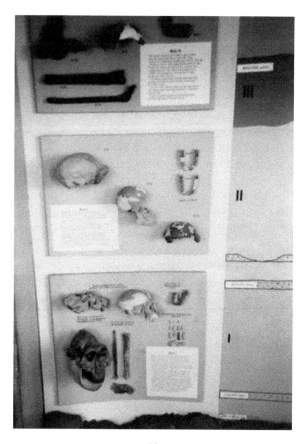

He went on to say that fossils, discovered in the Gorge, indicated that different types of early humans co-existed in East Africa. This put links in the theory of a single evolutionary chain. He continued by stating that, starting in 1926, Louis Leakey led expeditions there, where he found important fossils and stone tools. Mary Leakey, also a British

Paleoanthropologist and an expert in stone tools, joined Louis Leakey's expeditions and they married in 1936. Mary found the skull of

Australopithecus Boisei there in 1959. The find was said to be the first that showed the great antiquity of Hominids in East Africa.

Joe continued to say that, in 1960 the discovery of Homo Habilis, or "handy man" as he became known, was the first human who made and used stone and bone tools. Richard Leakey discovered a large number of Hominid fossils, including a number of skulls and other skeletal bones of very early representatives of modern humans. These included the earliest skull of Australopithecus. While the exact interpretation of the fossil finds was well debated, their significance to the field of physical anthropology was universally acknowledged.

He also mentioned that other fossil remains, unearthed in more recent times, provided further evidence that the genus Homo co-existed with other advanced man-ape forms, known as Australopithecines, up to three million years ago. Both of these Hominids appeared to be descendants of the three and a half million-year-old Australopithecus Afarensis. This ancestor of Homo had the legs and body for walking upright, thereby freeing the arms and hands to manipulate objects. Additional fossil arm and leg bone remains, thought to be nearly two million years old and discovered in the Olduvai Gorge, added further weight to the view that the Human evolutionary progress was quite uneven. However, the fossils, particularly those found in the "Castle" excavation, provided evidence of relatively advanced upright bipedal locomotion. At the end of the talk on the Gorge, we applauded the speaker and thanked him.

After I had finished my refreshments, I had a look around the Centre at the fossils and charts on the walls. The charts showed the places where the fossils had been found in the Gorge. I found this fascinating, as it was one of the places I had been longing to see.

I came out of the Visitors' Centre, and stood on the rim of the Gorge, looking across at what looked like a plateau from an American Western film.

That was where the fossils, which I had looked at in the Visitors' Centre, were discovered. I thought Joe called it the "Castle", but it looked more like a scene from a John Wayne cowboy film. I think it was because of the reddish colour of the rock and its stratification. Having looked at the charts in the Visitors' Centre, showing where the fossils were found, I could imagine which strata contained the fossils by just looking at the "Castle".

Back in the land rovers, and driving to our new campsite on the Serengeti Plain, I had joined Sid, Mark and Maureen in their land rover. This was partly because Sid's wife had swapped with me, so she could chat to the two ladies, Connie and Enid, in Rusty's land rover. It was also because I wanted to ask Sid more about evolution. From our chat in the garden of the Impala Hotel in Arusha, I found out that he had a particular interest in Anthropology. This was the area of the trip to which he was looking forward. I had, therefore, asked Sid to explain more about Homo Habilis.

"Just imagine Karl" Sid said, "Twenty million years ago this part of East Africa was a vast plateau covered in forest. At that time, a particular species of Dryopithecine roamed in these wooded areas, collecting plants and seeds as they fed on the rough vegetation. This was a Miocene ape, known as Ramapithecus. Although it was more ape-like than human-like, it was thought to be the evolutionary ancestor of man."

"Sounds interesting", I said, "please go on, I'm very interested in this". Sid continued. "This plateau was created when the earth's crust rose up into a huge dome, giving rise to massive volcanoes which erupted, spewing out rivers of molten lava. The sheer pressure, forcing up minerals from the bowels of the earth's core, caused the dome to split creating a wide valley.

The dome continued to swell and widen, as the split in the earth's crust spread towards the coast. At the coast the Indian Ocean rushed in, cooling the lava flows down and leaving a giant inland sea. As centuries went by the earthquakes, which continued to rage in this unstable land, broke up the inland sea into large and small lakes, surrounded by plateau and high mountains. Some of the lakes were very rich in minerals and, consequently, had large amounts of soda dissolved in them. This made them into, what has become, a haven for wildlife. As the lava flows cooled and shrank, and the earthquakes subsided in their intensity, a great rift valley was left. This Great Rift Valley's eco-environment stabilised allowing fauna and flora to flourish on its upper slopes, together with the life that depends on it".

"What happened to the ape-man Sid?" I asked, as he settled back into his seat in the land rover. "Well Karl, the northern highlands of Tanzania of which, as you know, Mount Kilimanjaro and Mount Meru form part, provide an ideal habitat for a wealth of wildlife of every description. The rainfall on these mountain slopes is high, refreshing the lush vegetation and creating streams, and eventually torrential rivers flowing into the lowlands below these majestic peaks. Further south part of the rim of this great rift valley is formed from volcanoes, which encompass craters such as the Calderas of Ngorongoro, where we have just stayed. These Highlands overshadow the hot savannah grasslands of the valley floor, such as around Lake Manyara and beyond."

"It was on these newly-formed savannah grasslands that the evolutionary ape-like creatures settled, around the lakes, rivers and streams. Here they further developed their skills in hunting, and also developed tools they could use to exploit the resources of the area. This evolution has been well documented by Doctor Leakey since 1926. However, confusion still persists over this complex area of science, although it is thought two kinds of hominid creature evolved from Ramapithecus in this area of East Africa. Ramapithecus, or Australopithecus Afarensis as it became known, was the earliest ape-man of nearly three and a half million years ago, which evolved into Australopithecus Africanus nearly two and a half million years ago. Australopithecus Africanus evolved into two types of creature, depending on where they resided. Australopithecus Robustus continued to live on the upper slopes of the rift valley, feeding on plants and fruits in the rich rainforests. They, therefore, evolved with the development of a large jaw, and back teeth to grind the fibrous material".

Sid continued, "The other creature, Homo Habilis, evolved as some of the Australopithecus Africanus moved from the highlands to the savannah grasslands, to hunt animals as a source of food. They, therefore, developed canine teeth in their powerful jaws, to tear at the flesh as they had evolved into meat-eaters. In order for him to survive such a hostile environment, he had to develop cunning and weapons to track and corner his prey, in order to make a kill. His more erect posture enabled him to run more easily across the open grasslands, and cover greater distances". I thanked Sid for this information, as I was particularly interested in this area of evolution.

The land rovers carried on towards the Serengeti National Park Gate, through the open savannah that surrounds it.

"Who found the Gorge, Sid?" I asked. "I remember reading something about it in the Visitors' Centre". He reflected and said, "The Maasai call the Gorge 'Oldupai', or the place of the wild Sisal. This is a spiky plant that has many uses, such as an antiseptic, for rope or basket work, and also for clothes. We saw it near the trees which had the Weaver Birds' nests hanging from them, earlier in the trip. Oldupai was discovered by Wilhelm Kattwinkle, a neurologist who was studying Sleeping Sickness in this part of Africa. He also had a particular interest in Palaeontology, so he was also looking for fossils and discovered them in the Gorge."

Sid went on to talk about the study of the material remains of past human life, and other researches concerned with the past. He also said that the research findings no longer appear to be the case, as existing scientists have been turning their attention to material cultures, and the products of these cultures, such as urban waste and landfills. Therefore, current thinking is linked to many other fields. For instance, techniques such as radiocarbon dating, developed by Atomic Physicists, or techniques for evaluating fauna developed by Palaeontologists, to name but a few.

At that point in our conversation, we were interrupted by George, our driver, who stopped as he had seen something on the track. It turned out to be a Chameleon crossing the track. We all got out of the land rover to take a photograph of it, while George picked it up with a stick for us to get a closer look.

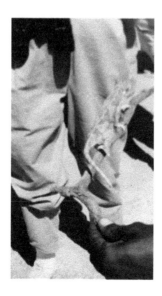

We continued on our way to the Serengeti National Park Gate.

Chapter 10

Roaming the Serengeti

George told us that the Serengeti National Park was established in nineteen fifty-one and boasts the greatest concentration of plains animals in Africa. Herds of Wildebeest, Zebra, Gazelle, Elephants, Rhino and Buffalo roam the plains, along with Lions, Leopards, Cheetahs, Hyenas, Jackals, Hippos, Primates, and over two hundred species of Birds. It covers over five and a half thousand square miles, stretching from Arusha right up to Lake Victoria, with nearly a quarter of its land set aside as Reserve. I had heard that Tanzania has one of the best conservation records on the Continent of Africa.

Having passed the Serengeti National Park gate entrance, we ventured further onto the Plains which, at that point, seemed very flat.

Topi and Secretary Bird

Figure 22 Secretary Bird

What should appear, "out of the blue", but a Secretary Bird strolling across the grass. It was probably looking for the snakes it feeds on. This was an exciting sighting for me, as I had always wanted to see one of those, more than any other bird.

We ventured a little further, and I could see a group of Topi grazing in front of one of the first rocky outcrops we had seen. The rocky outcrops were scattered all over the area, and called Kopje. They support a whole host of wildlife, giving them shade as they often have trees and shrubs on them.

Shortly after I could see another Kori Bustard, just before we turned off to view a small Hippo pool. There were about half a dozen Hippos in the pool, and they were closer to us than the ones we saw in the Crater. We passed a couple of Giraffe feeding on some thorn bushes.

Finally, we arrived at one of the Seronera camp sites, one of a number in the area which consisted of tents. Having put our belongings into our allocated tents, and after a swift meal, we were off looking for a Leopard. We decided to separate the land rovers so that we could cover a wider area.

Our land rover entered a wooded area near our campsite, and we spotted a number of other vehicles parked near some long grass. George parked alongside them. The people in them were observing a Leopard peering out of the long grass.

^
Leopard

Figure 23 Leopard

I could see its head and shoulders clearly visible, but it was just sitting there, only moving its head about.

One of the other observers, from the other vehicles told us that they had been tracking the Leopard for half an hour, as it stalked a herd of Topi. It had not caught one, and had just plonked itself down in the grass. I tried to take a photo of it, but my camera was not good enough to get as clear a view as my naked eye, especially in the fading light. After a while we left and continued to look around the wooded area, to see if we could find another Leopard in a tree, as this would be the classic place to find one. We could not find one, but were pleased by our sighting of the one in the long grass, and we then went on to meet up with the other members of the group.

Having met up with the other land rovers, we all went back into the wooded areas to try and find another Leopard. The other groups were unlucky and had not seen a Leopard. We could not find any more, but could see lots of Topi and Green Vervet Monkeys, and decided to go back to Camp for the night.

At five in the morning, I was awoken by roaring Lions, and people were wandering around the camp with flashlights. I had had a good night's sleep, but that was not surprising as yesterday had been a long, tiring day. I got up and dressed, and tried to take a photo of the beautiful dawn breaking., but I didn't think I would do it justice. At seven o'clock, I went to the Mess Tent to await breakfast. I felt hungry as usual, and put it down to all the fresh air and exercise I was getting.

Near the kitchen area was a large pit into which to tip the rubbish, but this was surrounded by a troop of Baboons who were noisily defending their territory, and challenging each other like a gang of kids playing "king of the castle".

I watched one large, fearsome looking male, who seemed to dominate the mound around the pit. The younger males were taunting him and, in doing so, he was becoming angrier and angrier and chasing off their challenges. As he chased off one of the younger males, the others rushed into the pit and pinched some of the fruit dumped there. I quickly recognised that these Baboons were not like the ones in the Crater, instead they came closer to people as if unafraid of them. I thought that they had obviously become used to people, because they had probably rummaged on the tip for years. Even so, I was fascinated by the entertainment they provided, and realized I could venture closer to them to take a photograph, without them running away. I was, therefore, able to take photograph of them before going back into the Mess tent to have my breakfast.

After breakfast we drove out again, looking for more wildlife. I saw some more of those fascinating Secretary Birds, and lots of smaller birds which I could not recognize. However, in one tree I did see four Lesser Kestrels perched on the branches. We came across a group of rocks, where a number of Hyrax were scurrying about. These creatures looked quite appealing, with their terrier-like faces and small plump bodies, about the size of a rabbit. We did not see any more Leopards, from the six pairs believed to be in the area.

There was a group of Green Vervet Monkeys, about twenty yards from the land rover. A male was sitting on a log, watching others playing in a dip behind him. Amongst them were some mothers with their young.

As we followed the river bed, to our surprise, there was plenty of water in it. We came across three more Vervet Monkeys, by the left-hand side of the track, with a large Giraffe over to our right. It was getting warmer as the sun was rising higher in the sky, although it was fairly cloudy. It was certainly much hotter than it had been on the Crater floor, which I supposed was at a higher altitude. As we moved along the river bank, we came across deeper pools of water surrounded by luscious undergrowth, with palms and reeds making it an attractive sight. Some of the group had spotted a Monitor Lizard, about six feet long but, disappointingly, I could not see it although I had seen one on television.

Moving further along the track we observed two Lionesses, heading straight towards us. One of them passed very close to my land rover, and looked straight up at me.

I was relieved that she decided not to leap into the land rover, but it was incredible to have such close eye contact with one of these marvellous beasts.

Figure 24 Bateleur Eagle

Close by I spotted a Bateleur Eagle, in a tree.

Out into the open area of grassland, with a nice breeze in my face, I saw a couple of Warthogs, running across the track in front of us, and off towards a group of six Giraffe to our right. The Warthogs were running fairly swiftly away from us, but seemed unconcerned about us being there. About fifty yards in front, a Mongoose walked out onto the track. It took one look at us and walked back into the long grass, from the direction it had come. We slowed down a little because of this incident, and I could see two Crowned Cranes standing over to my right, where there were some Topi. We paused for a while to observe these.

Heading back towards the wooded area, a rather large Warthog shot across in front of us, from out of the long grass. Luckily, we just missed it. Approaching the wooded area, there were lots more Giraffe, including one mother with her two small calves. Close by were two large males, standing near some trees. I could also see several Griffon Vultures, perched on the trees. There were more Topi on the track and more Warthogs behind them, surrounded by quite a large group of magnificent Impala, with their impressive horns standing out against the bushes behind.

Impala

Further down the track through the wooded area, as we moved back towards the camp, I saw more Topi on both sides of us, and a large herd of Impala which consisted of around fifty in number.

Figure 25 Oryx

A large Oryx was lying under a tree not far from the track side and, in fact, everywhere I looked I saw wildlife thriving in this rich grassland.

Chapter 11

Visit to the Seronera Wildlife Lodge

By four o'clock we were back in camp, ready to use the camp showers that had been erected for us by the camp staff.

These consisted of a bucket, with a spray nozzle on the bottom of the bucket, and a chain to open and close the tap. The bucket was suspended from a tree, and surrounded by a blue tarpaulin.

The ladies went first, while the gentlemen disappeared into their tents. Unfortunately, one of the ladies pulled the chain too hard, and the whole contraption came down on top of her. I could hear quite a bit of hilarity from the other ladies, as the camp staff tried to repair it, whilst the lady tried to preserve her modesty. We all took it in turn to use the showers, me being one of the last. I walked across with my small towel around me, while all of the others were in their tents, getting ready to go out to visit the exclusive

Seronera Wildlife Lodge.

After our refreshments we got into the land rovers again, and drove past the Hippo pool, only this time one Hippo was out of the water.

Because of the danger, we stayed in the land rovers to photograph the Hippo.

Along the river bank I saw a Crocodile in the water, just beneath the surface.

Moving further on, we passed more Giraffe and Warthogs, and some Reedbuck. The Reedbuck bounced across the ground, as they moved away from our land rover. The weather was still hot, with an increasing number of rain clouds forming. In fact, it was very dark over in the distance, where it actually looked like it was raining. Luckily it was fine where we were, just on the edge.

As we approached another pool in the river, we spotted two more Crocodile floating just beneath the surface.

I saw two Crested Cranes looking down from a nearby tree, so we stopped for a moment to watch them, before moving towards the bridge across the river. The bridge was taking us to our destination, the Seronera Wildlife Lodge. As we crossed the bridge, I could see more Crocodile in the water, and one of them was quite large.

We arrived at the Seronera Wildlife Lodge, set on top of and around a rocky outcrop called a Kopje.

The Lodge was built in such a way that the corridors were set into the rocks as part of the complex.

We entered the complex, and were met by a group of Rock Hyrax, who greeted us in the corridor. They were quite tame and used to people, so we were able to get quite close to photograph them.

I went up the stairs of the Lodge, and through the bar at the back onto a veranda, where I got a very good view across the Serengeti Plain from the excellent vantage point. I easily observed lots of animals grazing, although it was getting darker. After some refreshment in the bar, we made our way back to the land rovers, through an army of Marabou Stork which were parading like dinosaurs in the twilight.

I felt uneasy as I made my way across the track, weaving between the Marabou Stork, as they seemed as tall, if not taller, than me.

The sun was sinking, creating a giant orange glow in the sky now that the rain clouds had dispersed. As the sun made way for the night, it became more difficult to see. Marabou Stork were flying around us, preparing to settle for the night. Behind me, in the trees near the bar, Hyrax were nibbling at the leaves. It was nearly dark by the time we got back to the land rovers. Driving back to camp we saw a number of Owls, and other creatures of the night which were not easily identifiable.

Back in camp we had a late meal, before venturing out again at 9.30 pm, to find some of the night life nearby. It was a short stroll down the track, to watch what has become a daily event. That was the silent lightening over Lake Victoria. Silent because of the distance it was from us. However, it was still fascinating to watch. The noise made by the nocturnal insects filled the air, and occasionally we heard a roar from some of the Lions. We met up with a man who had a sound recording of an Owl which he was studying. He played the recording and the Owl, which he was attracting, appeared. As he shone his light on the Owl, it turned its head and, amazingly, had a face on the back of it. He told us that it was for the Owl's defence against predators, as the predators thought the owl was looking at them. Fascinating!!

Chapter 12

In Search of the Elusive Cheetah

I awoke at seven o'clock, and another fine day greeted me, although to be honest I felt somewhat cold, and I felt cold in the night in the tent. Rusty had put his coat over the top of his bed, so he was still snuggled down asleep. That was because he had more sense than me. I had just heard that Bob had been unwell in the night, so I popped in to see him to offer some tea and sympathy, although I thought he might decline the tea. As a matter of fact, a couple of days ago I had also been unwell, and, so had most of the party since we came to Africa. The exception were those members of the group who had travelled extensively in the climate before. It seemed as if it was expected, and we had all brought appropriate medication with us, in addition to the jabs and anti-malarial treatment we were taking. That alone may have caused our problems, although our diet had been rich in fruit and vegetables. Even so, like everyone in the camp, Bob was determined to go out in search of the elusive Cheetah. Apparently, over three hundred yards, it can sprint up to seventy miles per hour, so I hoped we could see one before it ran away! Excitement was stirring as we ate our breakfast, and waited to leave camp.

Just after nine o'clock, we made our way onto the Serengeti again, in search of what is the world's fastest land mammal, the Cheetah!

Figure 26 White-headed Buffalo Weaver

As we left camp, we could clearly see a White-headed Buffalo Weaver, with its white neck and chest, orange rump and dark brown wings.

We also saw a Blue-eared Glossy Starling. Everywhere we looked, as far as the eye could see, there was a carpet of green, covered in wall-to-wall animals. I understood from the literature I had read, and from various television programmes, that it was at that time of year that these great herds of animals made their way through the obstacles from Kenya, to graze on the vast plain and produce their next generation. I was not disappointed with what I saw. Scattered all around me were mother Wildebeest with their young, as well as Zebra and Antelope. Food was plentiful, so it was the right time for them to have their offspring. There were some Thomson's Gazelle over to my left, with the tiniest young I had ever seen in my life. Some Zebra were over to my right, also with their young. The picture was idyllic.

As we ventured further and further into the grasslands, we came across herds of cattle tended by the Maasai. Some of the Maasai were carrying spears, I presumed to ward off predators. What struck me more was the harmony between the people living on the vast savannah, and the wild animals which roamed there. It seemed like there was a kind of mutual respect or trust between them. As we passed yet more herds of animals, such as Impala, our driver, Hussain, pointed out that the males had the horns while females did not, and at that time of year they fight for territory.

We travelled onto the Central Plains, which gave the appearance of the flat prairies of the old wild west of America. The weather was hot again, with the sun fairly high, and the dry grass was seeding. I could see for miles and miles, with only the Kopjes (rocky outcrops) to break up the view. Here there were very few animals to be seen, and the only trees were in the vicinity of the rocks.

We decided that we would visit some of the rocky outcrops to see if we could find any animals there, sheltering from the heat of the day. We entered one where we saw several Eagles flying around, and others were perched on the branches.

On another rocky outcrop we saw two male Lions, basking in the hot sun. Hussain told us that the one at the foot of the rock was about fourteen years old, which was unusual because lions generally only live for twelve years. I noticed that one of them had a collar, something I had not seen before. Hussain said that the Lion must have been part of a Research Project.

Soon we were off the beaten track, looking for the shy, elusive Cheetah. We were told that they would be difficult to find in that vast area. As we moved nearer to another group of rocky outcrops to our right, near the side of the track was a Golden Jackal. We saw several lizards on the rocks. Around the area there were lots and lots of Zebra and Antelope, so we were more optimistic that we would soon be seeing some Cheetah.

Luck was on our side. We came across a lone, pregnant Cheetah laid in the grass. It was purely by chance because, at first, we could hardly see her, then she got up and walked away from us. We circled around her so as not to alarm or stress her unduly, and we were still able to photograph her from a good distance, before we moved on towards more rocks. Hussain told us that fifty per cent of Cheetah cubs die in the first three months, and we were lucky to see the cheetah, especially in the open savannah.

Moving further towards more rocky outcrops, we found one large isolated rock which had a Lioness laid on the top of it.

There were several large Lizards lower down. Some were at least twelve inches long. They were blue and orange in colour, and Hussain told us they were Agama lizards.

Figure 27 Agama Lizard

The rocky outcrops provided shelter from the very hot sun of midday. It was soon time to pause for a picnic lunch, so we moved around the rocks towards a sheltered spot. Someone had beaten us to it!! Laid in the grass, under the shade of an Acacia tree, were two magnificent male Lions with the same idea as us.

We moved quickly to a safer picnic spot and, as we did, we saw some more Tawny Eagles and some Vultures. To our surprise a troop of Baboons were heading in the Lions' direction. "What a shock they will have when they get around the corner," I thought. The snacks and refreshments were very welcome, as we sat on a fallen tree trunk and enjoyed them, in the welcome shade of an Acacia tree, well away from the Lions. Looking out from the rocky outcrop we saw large herds of Zebra, and Antelope such as Thompson's and Grant's Gazelle, and Topi.

It was after one o'clock, and we set off to see more of the rocky outcrops. It was very hot as we drove back across the green grasslands of the wider plains, where the thousands and thousands of Wildebeest and Zebra grazed.

At first, they seemed like spots on the horizon but, as the convoy drew closer, Hussain shouted for everyone to look over to the right to see the herds of Wildebeest in the distance. I was amazed! There were literally, and I mean literally, thousands and thousands of Wildebeest grazing on the vast plains. These massive herds had come down from the Masai Mara in Kenya, to feed on the rich grasslands there, and to have their offspring. Hussain told us that up to a million Wildebeest migrate, with about half a million Zebra, to the rich grasslands. I had read somewhere that the Wildebeest were known as the "lawn mowers" of the Serengeti, spending a third of the day "clipping" the grass, and depositing "fertilizer" on the Savannah. It was after two o'clock when we made our way along the track, through the herds of animals, and onward to the central southern end of the Serengeti, and the Naabi Hill.

Naabi Hill is the largest of the Kopjes, at the southern end of the Serengeti. After leaving the Hill, we saw a couple of adult female Ostriches, with about twenty young, running away to the front of us. It was quite a sight, like two child minders and a nursery full of baby Ostriches. I saw a Secretary Bird with the Naabi Hill behind, and a dead Zebra covered in Vultures. The Vultures were squealing and squawking as they, in pecking order, took their fill of the carcass. Hussain thought the Zebra must have died rather than have been killed, because of the wholeness of it, and there was no sign of other larger predators near it. Further on we came across more Gazelle and Zebra, three Kori Bustards displaying and, to our surprise, Banded Mongooses on a termite mound about twenty yards from the land rover. We were going back into the wooded areas looking for a Leopard, when a Slender Mongoose ran across the track in front of us. It was quite characteristic, with the black tip on its tail. We did not find another Leopard, therefore headed back to camp.

Back in camp, I stood in front of my tent looking out at the evening twilight, and I noticed several bats flying around me. The sun had set over the horizon, and the campfire light had taken over from it. It had been a pleasant evening, and I had spent most of it sitting with some of the others, around the campfire, chatting about the day's events. Earlier I visited Bob, because he had been feeling unwell again. In myself, I was feeling much better, and could take solid food again, although I was tired and looking forward to a good night's sleep. It was the last night under canvas, as we were going to Ndutu Lodge the next day.

Chapter 13

Leaving the Serengeti by the Naabi Hill Gate

Having tossed and turned throughout the night as I did not find camp beds very comfortable, I was looking forward to a more comfortable bed at the Ndutu Lodge. People had been moving about a lot, perhaps they had been restless too. There were also a lot of strange wildlife noises, some of which we thought were Hyena. I had read somewhere that there were lots of Hyena on the Serengeti, some packs having over eighty in number. They hunted at night, and made a weird noise which sounded as if they were laughing. They are intelligent and skilful hunters, and can eat a third of their weight in one meal, with a crushing bite that exerts a force of up to a thousand pounds!! They eat everything, the bones, the teeth, everything, so you wouldn't want to be on the end of one of those animals, or rather front!

We headed out to leave the Serengeti at the Naabi Hill Gate, and to go to the Ndutu Lodge to stay the night. I had found out, through our discussions around the campfire the previous night, that we had been to the Gol Kopjes, and to the Retima Hippo Pool. The reason given for us not seeing lots of Leopards and Cheetahs was that they were solitary animals, and not often found in groups.

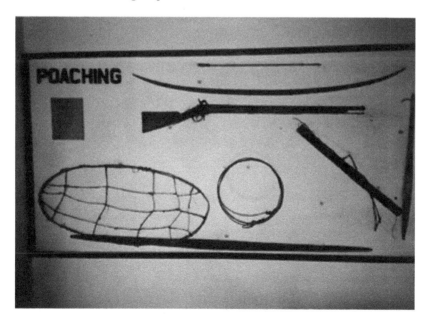

Apparently, poaching is a real problem on the Serengeti, and other Parks, as we found out when we called in at the Park's Wardens' Museum. There we saw a gun, nets, and even a bow and arrow, which the Wardens had confiscated.

One other thing that was really noticeable was the tremendous variety of butterflies and insects around. I have already mentioned the small Praying Mantis on the lamp, which caught a Gnat as I watched it. Some of the beetles I saw, like the Dung Beetle, were enormous by my home country standards. Mosquitoes were a problem there, so I had taken protection with me, such as sprays and creams. I took two types of anti-malarial tablets, because of the different strains of Malaria I might have been facing. These were recommended by my doctor. Where appropriate, I wore long-sleeved shirts, particularly when I sat out at night with the rest of the group.

As we left the Seronera area we came across a large Warthog, attempting to cross in front of our land rover, but it decided to wait until we passed.

There were several varieties of animal, including Topi and Warthog, a bird called a Rock Chat, and an abundance of Swallows. It seemed that many of our migratory birds flew to Africa during our Winter, and one of these was the Swallow. We saw these all around us. I was sure that there were many other species that had migrated from Britain which I had noticed but, because I was looking for unusual birds that I had not recorded before, I had not registered them. I saw lots of highly coloured local birds, which I did not recognise because of my lack of knowledge. I was, therefore, dependent upon the tour leader, and other members of the birdwatching group, to identify them.

We headed for the Ndutu Lodge, about fifty miles away, via the Naabi Hill Gate. As we approached the Gate, we saw a couple of male Lions amongst the Wildebeest. As they might have been hunting, we did not stop and disturb them. At the Gate, and in the building close by, were two Barn Owls in the underdrawing of the roof. Tom pointed them out to me, as they flew across the beams, and I could see them with my binoculars, through his torchlight which caught their white wings and bodies.

As I waited outside the building, ready to move on, I knocked over some small rocks with my foot, looking for insects. Tom came over to me, and made a point of telling me not to kick over the rocks, in case there was something nasty under them. I had not really thought about it, because it was a habit from my childhood, when looking for insects in the woods and fields. I felt embarrassed but, at the same time, grateful for his intervention and thanked him. There were some venomous snakes about, which one would not like to have hanging onto one's foot.

We moved out of the Serengeti, and headed further south from the Gate. It was an area of very short sparse grass, but greener than we had passed through so far. There were a few smallish herds of Thomson's and Grant's Gazelle. The road was atrocious, with a grey-brown coloured surface, which was quite gravelly and very dusty. In fact, as we drove on, at around fifty miles per hour, stones were flying up, and we were creating a large dust cloud behind us. Fortunately, we were the lead vehicle so it was not so much a problem for us, but I felt sorry for those following. However, we had been in that situation before when another land rover was leading.

Occasionally, or every few hundred yards along the way, we saw a Montagu's Harrier or a Pallid Harrier, identified by Ernest with whom I was sharing the rover, rather than me. He told me that they were very similar birds, and could easily be mixed up. He said that they were small birds of prey, with the male having a light grey body and black-tipped wings, whilst the female was browner in colour. Every so often we would go over a rise and see a long procession of Wildebeest and Zebra, moving in the same direction. Behind them were more Gazelle.

Just passed the Ngorongoro conservation area gateway, sheltering under an Acacia tree, was a pack of four African Hunting Dogs.

We were about twenty yards away at first, but Hussain inched us closer. We waited a long while for the dogs to stir. As they sat up more, I could see their brownish-yellowish coats, large ears and vicious looking teeth. This was a very rare sighting of these dogs we were told. Again, how lucky we were!

Having driven on, we entered a wooded area where there were hundreds of Wildebeest and Zebra. Hussain said that they tended to roam around that area until May, when they moved back North. We travelled on until we reached the Ndutu Lodge for the night.

Chapter 14

Lakes Masek and Ndutu and our Walking Safari

I had, with the rest of the group, finally arrived at Ndutu Lodge, after spending more time observing the vast herds of Wildebeest and Zebra, grazing on the lush grasslands of the southern Serengeti.

The accommodation there was an African style hut, which was covered by a thatched rectangular roof, the whole building being enclosed by a straw wall. It had an open door and window to the front, facing the large Lakes Masek and Ndutu. The huts were set in a wooded area, which stretched down to the edge of the lakes.

Lake Ndutu

There were many Acacia trees covered with Weaverbird nests.

Weaver bird nests

The whole area was very flat, similar to the Serengeti and covered at that time of year with animals. Besides the Wildebeest, there were hundreds if not thousands of Zebra around the area, which had migrated from the North.

Having settled into the accommodation, we set off to explore the local area by land rover. Our journey took us to the edge of Lake Masek where we were to start our walking safari. Whilst driving through the wooded areas, we came across a stampede of animals.

We could just see the animals through the massive cloud of dust they were creating, and could hear the roar of their hooves. The animals mainly consisted of Wildebeest and Zebra. We waited until they passed, and I took a photograph of them. As we came closer to Lake Masek the weather was getting much cooler. This was a blessing as we were going to walk around the lake.

At the lakeside, the first thing that struck me was the abundance of Wildebeest carcasses, floating on the water. We were told by the Guide, who was taking us on the walk, that it was a soda lake and, therefore, there were not any Crocodiles around to eat the bodies of the animals. The Wildebeest got stuck in the mud when trying to cross the lake, on their migration south. Apparently, the Vultures would not touch them either, because of the soda in the water. At that time of year, the banks of the lake were quite dry, so scientists checked to see how many had died that year by collecting the skulls of the Wildebeest. I could see many piles of skulls on the banks, as we walked along the Lake's edge.

We walked on to Lake Ndutu, and came across some Flamingos, and other wading birds I could not identify. However, we had spotted a Peregrine Falcon diving past us, as we made our way through the rows of Acacia trees which surrounded that part of the lake.

We could not see any small creatures, although there were many tracks imprinted into the sandy soil and, alarmingly, an abundance of snake trails. Luckily there were no signs of the snakes that had made them. Our Guide told us that the snakes slithered away, once they felt the vibration of the ground. "Thank goodness for that", I thought. For our safety an armed Warden was escorting us, just in case there were any large predators around, such as Lions which feast on the abundance of animals there.

After the long walk, we went back to a well-deserved meal in camp.

That evening, as usual, we gathered around to discuss the day's events before retiring for the night. Throughout the tour, I tended to live by a "dawn and dusk" routine. As the nights were longer at that time of year, I had gone to bed early and risen early.

I awoke again early, to a cacophony of chatter from the Weaverbirds outside my window. They were fascinating to watch but hellishly noisy, as if they were arguing with each other all the time. It was already bright and very warm. I strolled across to the mess tent for breakfast just as the tractor came into the camp, pulling the water bowser containing our fresh supply for the day. There was a shortage of fresh water there, so we had to be sparing with how much we used. It was surprising how much we took it for granted back home. The other tourists, who were in camp with us, were already packed and waiting to set off on their trip to the Masai Mara. We were going to visit Lake Ndutu once again, after breakfast, to see the

Flamingos, Ringed Plovers, Black-winged Stilts and Grebes which were abundant on the lake. I noticed a sweet sickly smell in the air, like stale bread, but I could not work out what it was, or where it was coming from. Maybe it was from the lake and the floating, rotting carcasses.

Having boarded the land rovers, we set off for Lake Ndutu again, roughly to the area where we walked yesterday. We passed a group of walkers along the way, and waved to them as we passed. No more than three hundred yards further on were two Lionesses, lazing in the sun. We turned back to warn the walkers, before proceeding on our journey. They were grateful for our intervention, and thanked us for coming back to warn them, otherwise they would have walked straight into the "lion's den".

As we went further around the lake towards the wooded areas, we could see more birds, such as Black-necked Grebe, and a variety of vultures and other birds of prey. Arriving at the other side of the lake, we came across a minibus of people, observing a very large vulture. We exchanged greetings, and briefly discussed what we were doing. It transpired that they had stopped for a walk, only to find four Wild Hunting Dogs lying under a tree. I wondered whether they were the same ones that we had seen.

We set off once more, this time away from the lake area and surrounding woodlands, towards the flat plains. On our approach to the plains Hussain braked, and pointed towards something on the ground. I could not see to what he was pointing at first but, once he had got into a good position, I could see a Tortoise on the ground, fairly well camouflaged by the surrounding fauna. We were allowed to disembark from the land rovers to take a closer look at the find, once Hussain had considered the area safe. Hussain told us that it was a rare Leopard Tortoise.

Chapter 15

Meeting the Maasai Warriors

We crossed the Savannah and headed towards the Ngorongoro Crater rim once again. There were many species of wild animal there, some of which we had not seen in such numbers before. For example, we passed a family of Warthogs with eight young, all scurrying away as we drew nearer. We could also see a number of Ostriches with their young. In fact, everywhere in that area the animals seemed to have young.

As we moved higher up the Crater once again, we encountered large numbers of Giraffe, feeding on the thorn bushes. The area was scattered with Maasai, tending their cattle. They were armed to the teeth with sticks, knives and spears for their own protection, and to protect their revered cattle. We reached the Crater rim, and paused to eat our packed lunch, only to be approached by a group of five Maasai Warriors carrying sticks and spears. George, one of the other drivers, spoke to them, as we sat down beside them. They chattered away in their own ancient language, as we shared our packed lunches with them.

After we had finished our lunch, or rather, when they had finished our packed lunch, George suggested we had a dance and sing with them. So, some of us stood in a circle, and leaped up and down with our Maasai Warriors, to the rhythmic chant of a war dance so we were told.

George told us that Maasai were very superstitious, and therefore not keen on having their photograph taken. However, they agreed to pose for us, with the Ngorongoro Crater in the background. One thing I noticed was the quality and colour of the beads they were wearing which, together with their red cloaks, made them look very stately.

George told us that the social and economic life of the Maasai centred on livestock, such as cattle, sheep and goats, which provided meat and milk for a rich diet. Livestock herding was a practical way of life in the semi-arid climate, and terrain of the Great Rift Valley. To spare the environment, settlements were ideally moved from place to place.

Leaving the Maasai behind, we drove on to the Ngorongoro Crater Rim Lodge for a drink, before moving to Lake Manyara. The Lodge was set right on the top of the crater rim, with views overlooking the rainforest which surrounded the crater, and a view of the crater floor some two thousand feet below. As we sat on the lawn in the bright sunlight, sipping our refreshing drinks, the Manager, once again, came out to remind us not to leave the grounds in case there were predators about.

Around the rim of the crater the vegetation was very dense and green, with lush undergrowth. It was in contrast to the Serengeti, which was green at that time of year after the rains, but sparser than up on the crater walls. There were lots of trees with flowers, vines hanging down, palms scattered about, just how you would expect the jungle to be. There were plenty of animals and birds about, but it was difficult to spot them at a glance because of the cover and camouflage. There were Monkeys in abundance, in fact a whole array of wildlife was contained and maintained within that tropical rainforest. The only thing missing was Tarzan swinging out of the trees on one of the vines, using his distinctive "ululating" yell.

After leaving the Lodge, we made our way to the main entrance of the Crater, where we paused to allow the other land rovers to catch up. I was very tired and must have nodded off for a while, waiting for the others to arrive. As we set off again, a very large troop of Baboons came across the track in front of us, and I could see three very large males amongst them. We had to move off the track to let them pass. I estimated that there were around a hundred Baboons in the troop.

We went on towards the more fertile farmland. The rich, red coloured soil contrasted greatly against the bright green foliage. The road through that area was really rough, more a dirt track with big potholes along the way, tossing us about in the back of the land rover. We passed many farms, as the urban development encroached further up towards the rim of the Crater, taking advantage of the rich fertile land. We still saw Maasai herding their cattle, similar to the ones higher up the volcano. As we drove along the road, we threw up enormous clouds of dust, especially where we were going "off road" to avoid vehicles passing us. All the vehicles we met were four-wheel drive ones, or large trucks. The terrain was such that there seemed to be no cars suitable to negotiate it. As we drove further down the road, we could see Lake Manyara stretched out in front of us. We were going to stay near the Lake overnight, in African style Bandas.

The weather was very hot, as we arrived at our accommodation in the late afternoon. There was one Banda short, so four of us had to share, therefore, Tom and Bob joined Rusty and me. I offered Bob the bed, but he insisted that he slept on the floor, and proceeded to pile two mattresses on top of each other, next to my bed. I must say he looked rather cosy, whilst my bed felt like concrete had set in the mattress. After our meal, we chatted for a while before settling down for the night. There were Baboons surrounding the camp, and they were very noisy.

Chapter 16

Bird Haven on Lake Manyara

As usual, I awoke early to a potentially blistering day, as the temperature was already pretty high. Well, when I say that I awoke early, I really should say that I had not slept much at all, because I had tossed and turned on the very uncomfortable mattress. Overnight the Baboons had moved into the camp, covering every space between my Banda and the washroom. Bravely, I went out of the door, and wormed my way around and through them, clapping my hands and singing. Of course, with my singing voice they just stared at me, as if I was just some stupid human who had landed on their planet.

After breakfast we moved out to the entrance to Lake Manyara National Park, where Blue Monkeys were crossing the path near the gateway. We waited a while for our Driver, Mustafa, to check us into the park. It was eight o'clock by then and the temperature was already 30c.

Eventually we set off, and drove through the thick wooded areas at the foot of the Rift Valley wall. There were lots of Baboons on the ground, and Blue Monkeys in the trees.

Figure 28 Blue Monkeys

We passed over fresh water streams, and a river where a Kingfisher perched on a branch above it. Pelicans were nesting in the trees, and Hornbills were flying around them. Arriving on the bank of the lake, and looking out over the water, there was a plethora of birds and other wildlife which inhabited that magnificent salt lake.

Having parked our land rovers in a row, we faced the lake near the Hippo pool area. There were at least thirty Hippos partly submerged in the muddy water. I had never seen so many in one place before, so I was filled with excitement. That was another one of the things I had been longing to see. Beyond the pools stood thousands and thousands of Flamingo, Pelicans, Marabou Stork and Cormorants. They appeared too numerous to count and stretched for miles along the banks.

Figure 29 African Jacana

I could see a Jacana with its brown back, and white head with a stripe through its eye. It was walking on the lily pads, with its enormous feet having evolved for that purpose.

The sun was in front of us, but did not detract from the incredible sight of the thousands of birds spread out before us. The air temperature was well into the thirties, with only a few fluffy white clouds in the sky. The luminescent blue sky reflected on the lake, and on the fiery pink Flamingos, making it look as if the banks of the lake were burning.

Over to my right I could see the wall of the Rift Valley fading into the distance, and rising above the thick forests which covered its base. As we moved around the lake, I saw a couple of Giraffe standing in the track, facing each other with their necks crossed. They appeared to be barring us from entering the wooded areas, where we hoped to see the famous Tree Lions of Lake Manyara.

Leaving the lakeside, we entered the lightly wooded area, and got separated from the other land rovers. We halted because a dust storm had blown up from literally nowhere, and came across like a fog rolling in from the sea. It was an incredible sight to see the birds leaving the lakeside, and flying up above the red dust storm as it approached us. We had to get out of the land rover to put the canopy up, because the wind was becoming more intense. Sitting in the back of the land rover, and listening to the wind howling around us, while the dust and debris lashed against our canopy, we were forced into the decision to abandon our trip to see the Elephants. We were going to meet up with the others, but instead doubled back to the Hippo pools. We watched the animated Hippos, as they moved about more than we had seen before.

There were smaller birds flying over the pools as well. We could see Pied Kingfishers flying in, hovering, then dropping down to pick up small fish from around the edges of a pool. Swallows were also diving down to pick the flies off the surface of the pool. Between the Hippo pools and the main lake, there were herds of Zebra, Wildebeest and Gazelle. Another Jacana flew in, to land its giant feet on a large Lily pad, less than fifty yards from me.

Once the weather had cleared, we moved back to the wooded area, to see the famous Tree Lions of Lake Manyara. We were not disappointed, as we came across a lioness and her cub in one tree. At first, I had difficulty seeing them, despite them being pointed out to me by Mark. Eventually, I saw the lioness on a large branch in the centre of the tree, and her small cub higher up on the left. Rusty and I were sharing the land rover with Mark and Maureen Tyne that day. Mark was a keen photographer, and had the camera to get better close-ups of the Lions in the tree. The Lions' camouflage was excellent as they nestled in amongst the leaves.

Many of the trees in the area had some form of wildlife in them. I could see a Fish Eagle perched in one and, below it, a Turtle standing in the water near the edge of a stream. Nearby, a number of green Vervet Monkeys were sitting by the stream, as we made our way through the thick woodland.

We moved out into the more open areas, and came upon a lone Lioness, watching groups of Impala and Wildebeest. There were so many tourist vehicles around the area that she probably could not make a kill, even if she wanted to. After a while watching the animals, we headed back to camp for lunch. It was so hot, practically unbearable.

At two o'clock I was sitting in the shade of a Eucalyptus tree in camp, having had a cool shower on our return, and a snooze following lunch.

It was well over thirty-five degrees Celsius, even in the shade. I sat watching the Baboons, which seemed to permanently parade through the camp. I had got quite used to them, as they squabbled amongst themselves rather than bothering about us. They made such a racket. I saw half a dozen of them passing across in front of me, behind the tree in the middle of the camp site. The tree was about one hundred feet high, with a ten feet diameter trunk. In fact, we had seen some extremely varied and lush vegetation in the area, from Palm trees to enormous trees such as the one in front of me. As the weather was so hot, we decided not to go venturing out again, but to have a get-together instead in the camp. We enjoyed a relaxing afternoon, having a drink and talking about the morning's activities, especially seeing the tree lions.

The next day started with another of those glorious African mornings, vivid blue sky and bright warm sunshine. We were going to have a trip to the local village of Manyara and, after some shopping, we were going to visit the local Primary School to have a look around, and to give the children some gifts we had brought with us. When we arrived at the school, we were warmly welcomed by the Head Teacher, who thanked us for our gifts of pens, trinkets and sweets. He explained a little about the school.

The school was divided into seven classes, with one hundred and eighty students, ranging in age from seven years to fifteen years. The subjects included English, Swahili, Mathematics, Geography, History and Political Education. There were six teachers who each taught all the subjects on the syllabus.

We met some of the children in a classroom. They were writing with chalk on small chalkboards. They seemed pleased to see us, and welcomed our gifts. Afterwards we visited the teachers' quarters, including the Head Teacher's accommodation. Before leaving the school, we thanked the Head Teacher for his hospitality.

Leaving Manyara, we headed for the Tarangire National Park, which was famous for its hundreds of elephants.

Chapter 17

Elephants Galore in Tarangire

We continued through the gate into the Tarangire National Park after a brief pause, and headed towards the Tarangire camp where we were going to spend the night. Driving along, we bumped into a pride of Lions stalking some prey, so we stopped and waited while they moved off into the bush. We did not see them catch anything, but it was good to see them in the area. We also came across a group of Elephants, the animals we had specifically come to see.

Arriving at the Tarangire Safari Camp, six miles from the park gates, we were greeted by a row of two-man tents, each tent covered with a thatched canopy.

I did not think that we would be in tents any more, but these all had a flush toilet and shower at the back, behind each tent. The camp was originally built around nineteen-seventy, and was situated on top of a hill, overlooking the Tarangire National Park. To the front of our tent, and below the hill, was the nearly dried-up riverbed of the Tarangire river.

Through my binoculars, I could see animals going to and from the water's edge to drink. They were mainly Gazelle, but now and again an Elephant turned up. I could see many Oryx, Zebra and Gazelle sheltering under the Acacia trees. There was plenty of bird life around, such as Marabou Stork and colourful Bee-eaters. I was gradually beginning to learn some names for the birds, but many of these I could not identify by their individual names.

We had settled into our tents, and were enjoying a pleasant lunch. It was a buffet lunch consisting of meatballs, ham and chicken, of which we seemed to have had plenty during the week. We also had green beans, peas, cauliflower and carrots. There were always plenty of potatoes available as well. For sweet we had bananas, oranges, large sweet pineapples and mangoes, all of which I enjoyed. There was custard to go with it as well, and hot coffee to finish. The mango was a lovely, sweet fruit which I was not used to. It was much sweeter than the pawpaw. I had never had so much fruit and vegetables before. All healthy stuff. Not the sort of cuisine I had at home, because I lived on my own and could not be bothered to cook.

Once my lunch had settled, I decided to go for a swim in the raised concrete pool at the end of the tented area. The water in the pool was nice and cool, in contrast to the very hot air temperature. Although the pool was not very big, a few of us were able to cool off in the afternoon heat. I spent around an hour in the pool, splashing and diving around and felt great. It seemed I had managed to get the reputation of imitating "Moby Dick", the great white whale, because of my lack of bodily suntan. This was because I got burnt in Torquay back in the sixties, a painful experience. Whilst I was with the Army in Cyprus in nineteen-seventy-three, I was told that if you got sunburnt you would be put on a charge, so I had never bothered with it since.

We got ready again to go out in the land rovers at four o'clock, to look around the area. It was definitely cooler. Tom and Bob had been out to see some of the smaller birds, but they were back in the camp and raring to go again. In fact, the whole group went out for the evening drive.

We soon discovered an Oryx lying down in the grass, with several Hartebeest and Zebra about five hundred yards away from it. There was not a great deal of animals to see on the drive, except those already mentioned and a few Impala. The flies had pestered us all day, particularly the

Tsetse flies that seemed to go for the brown socks that I wore, constantly nipping my feet. Perhaps they mistook the socks for cowhide.

It was nearly six thirty when we returned to camp. The snow-capped peak of Kilimanjaro was clear in the distance, with Mount Meru visible as well. I got changed and decided to sit in front of my tent, looking over to the riverbed, waiting for supper.

That evening we had one of those wonderful sunsets you come to expect in the African wilderness. It consisted of a bright orange glow on the

horizon, behind the dark silhouettes of acacia trees. It was accompanied by the increasing sound of insects. Although I attempted to capture the moment, it was hard to do it justice, you had to be there to witness it for yourself. Beautiful!

I awoke to the dawn chorus, having had a very comfortable night. It was certainly a much cooler day as we set off in the land rovers to explore the park.

There were only Giraffe to see at first, then we came across the Elephants we were looking for. Three Elephants appeared, followed by another much larger one further on in a dip.

There were Dwarf Mongooses near a fallen tree, as we searched for more Elephants. A couple of lions appeared, but they looked really emaciated. We passed more Giraffe and, eventually, we came across a herd of around a dozen Elephants, but they were too far away. There were plenty of Ostrich and Impala to see as well. The Tsetse Flies were a nuisance, even worse than the previous day. There were thousands coming into the land rovers. Everybody had to cover up. We had bought square scarves in Manyara ready for the flies, but never expected it would be as bad as it was. The flies had gone for my ankles and feet again, feeling just like needles sticking into my skin. I was sorry I had only brought the brown woollen socks with me. Mind you that's all I had. Trust my luck for the flies to think they were animal skin. This was a place I would not forget in a hurry because of the damned flies!

At last, we found the Elephants!! Yes, at least a hundred Elephants around a waterhole. There was a large Bull Elephant amongst them.

Some of the Elephants were in the water, spraying it around and rolling in the mud.

As we moved nearer along the track, a very large Bull Elephant stood in our way.

At first its trunk was up and its ears were sticking out, poised to charge. Its tusks looked intimidating. Of course, we stopped dead and waited, wondering whether it would charge or not. Luckily it backed down and just walked away, much to our relief. We moved closer to the herd. One large Elephant was rubbing itself against a tree, while some other, much smaller ones, were rolling in the mud at the edge of the waterhole, including several young ones. Moving further on, we saw two more large herds of Elephants on either side of the track, at some distance from us. Near the river, we came across two Cheetah sitting on the bank. I could see them clearly through my binoculars, but they were too far away for my camera.

As we came across another herd of Elephants, they started to circle, the matriarchs on the outside, the young in the middle.

Their ears were stretched out, trunks in the air trying to sense us and, at the same time, trying to protect their young. No bull Elephants here. Mustafa told us that they tended to wander off from the herd, into the forests and hills. Sometimes they wandered for miles away from the herd. Overall, we saw around five hundred Elephants in the area.

We finally arrived at the bridge over the river, on our way back to Camp, and we paused for a while as a large Leyland bus passed us, carrying a party of school children. The children cheered and shouted as they went by, and we waved back at them. I wondered if some of them remembered us from our visit to the school.

Our next port of call was a fairly extensive swampy area, with lush long grass and pools of water in it. In some of the pools were Ducks, Stork and more African Jacanas. A couple of Marsh Harriers flew over the swamp, as well as a Blue-cheeked Bee-eater. As we moved further into the swampy area, the land rover came to a sudden halt, throwing us all forward into a heap on the floor. As I got up, Mustafa was quite excited and pointed to a snake, just disappearing into the dense undergrowth. I just caught a glimpse of it, but Mustafa got a full view of the snake as he drove around the bend in the track.

Figure 30 Spitting Cobra

Mustafa said that it reared up in front of the vehicle, and he identifed it as a Spitting Cobra. Apparently, this snake could spit its deadly venom up to thirty feet into the eyes of its victim. "A lucky escape" I exclaimed! The others agreed. We thanked him for his quick thinking. It was actually the first snake I had seen in the flesh, although we did see plenty of tracks in the sandy soil around Lake Ndutu where we walked. We gathered ourselves together and headed back to camp for lunch.

People were tired and, because of the heat of the day, we went back to camp early. It was our last day there, and we were going back to Arusha the next morning. It had been a wonderful day, especially seeing the hundreds of Elephants in their natural surroundings. It had also been special for me by seeing the two Cheetah. The rest of the group were pleased with their bird sightings as well.

Chapter 18

Strange Encounter in the Heat of the Sun

People were tired after the morning drive, so we all decided to rest for the afternoon. I decided to sit and relax in front of the tent, overlooking the riverbed where I could watch the animals coming to drink. Through my binoculars I could see Waterbuck, Impala and Giraffe. It was very pleasant sitting there surveying the valley below. To my right about ten yards away, there was a Woodpecker on the ground, pecking away at something.

Figure 31 African Green Woodpecker

I thought it was an African Green Woodpecker and, although my knowledge was improving all the time, I felt that I was doing well identifying it as a woodpecker. There were lots of little birds around as well, brightly coloured ones, blues, greens, turquoise and more. It really was a beautiful sight.

The children we had seen on the Leyland bus that morning were all in the swimming pool. I could hear them from five hundred yards away, so I decided to wait before I went for my swim and do my "Moby Dick" impression again. Instead, I decided to have a snooze. Rusty had already gone down to sit by the pool, so I was all alone and feeling at peace. However, it was a very warm afternoon and I could see Elephants walking towards the river bed. I watched for a while before my eyes closed.......

I opened my eyes wide, startled by a noise coming from behind the bushes to my right. My tent was at the end of the row, so there was nothing to my right except for the rubbish bins, twenty yards away. I thought it was one of the Baboons that had come to the garbage bins, but I could see a creature which was much taller and leaner. It was making a funny grunting sound as it searched through the bins, throwing the bin lids all over the place, with such a clatter. I must admit I was a bit shaken by the incident and somewhat apprehensive, so much so that I retreated into my tent and closed the flap behind me. Having laid low for a while, I bucked up enough courage to peer out of the tent, once the noise had subsided. To my amazement I caught a glimpse of the creature running down the hillside, towards the wooded area at the bottom of the hill. Reaching for my binoculars, I focused on the creature as it dashed through the bush, down towards the river, startling a large Marabou Stork on the way and, totally ignoring the Elephants now gathered at the waterhole.

Figure 32 Marabou Stork and Homo Habilis

The creature definitely did not look like a Baboon. However, to describe it, it was around five feet tall, dark brown hairy body, completely naked so causing me to exclude a human, although I did think it was more like a human than an ape or large monkey. It was the way it could run upright. Was I seeing Homo Habilis, or not??!!

Emerging from the tent, to get a closer look from the top of the hill, I bumped into Rusty, returning from the poolside. "What do you think Rusty?" I asked, handing him the binoculars. "What am I looking at?" he asked, as I pointed towards the river bed below us. "Can't you see that creature heading towards the river?", but by then the creature was obscured by the bush. "I can see some Elephants at the waterhole and some Antelope", Rusty replied. "NO, by the bush in the foreground" I exclaimed! "I can see a Marabou Stork, in front of the bush" replied Rusty.

Feeling embarrassed by my outburst, I remarked that it must have been one of those I saw. "Weird creatures those birds", Rusty replied, and picked up his towel and went for a shower. I continued to focus my binoculars on the river bed, hoping to get another glimpse of the creature. It wasn't to be, because the creature had disappeared into oblivion. Disappointed, I sat back in my chair, to contemplate what I had seen, and must have drifted back off to sleep.

The next thing I knew, Rusty woke me up when he returned from the poolside, and told me he had come for his towel, and was going for a shower before dinner. Confused, I got up from my chair, feeling a bit dizzy, with a bit of a headache from the heat of the sun. In front of me, I could see a group of Elephants approaching the waterhole, near the river bank. "What about the creature?" I asked myself. "Was it Homo Habilis, spooking me ever since I visited the Olduvai Gorge, or was it a dream I had? It must have been!!!" I picked up my towel, and went and replaced the bin lids, before heading to the shower to clear my head before dinner.

Chapter 19

Return to Arusha and Lake Duluti Jungle Hike

We were returning to Arusha, and were to lose the land rovers. In the afternoon we were to have a specially arranged walk around Lake Duluti, a volcanic crater lake which was surrounded by thick jungle.

The road back to Arusha took in the Italian road again, with magnificent views of snow-capped Kilimanjaro in the distance. We passed more Maasai villages along the way. My understanding was that the new road was being built to take the sulphur from the factory in Tarangire to Arusha. Unfortunately, our driver, George, had run out of petrol, and we waited with him for the other land rovers to catch up with supplies. So, whilst we waited, Rusty took a photo of me standing in some scrubland, with snow and cloud covered Mount Kilimanjaro in the background. Although the weather was quite hazy, I could just make it out.

Eventually, the others came and refuelled our land rover. They had stopped for a while on the way to also take photographs. We were soon on our way again, refreshed with a cool drink they had brought with them, for us.

As we arrived nearer to Arusha, Mount Kilimanjaro was virtually covered in cloud. Banana plantations lined either side of the road, and we saw many of the local people about. The houses were made from concrete block walls, with a tin roof on them. As we went further into the town, the road was lined with small shops, many selling fruit. George told us where to go to shop for the best bargains. At this point, after a little shopping, we bid farewell to our drivers. I gave the drivers a bottle of whisky which I had purchased on the aeroplane coming over. This was mainly because I was not a whisky drinker, and everybody seemed to have brought a bottle with them as well. I thought it was recommended, to drink around the camp fire. I also gave them my Tanzanian Shillings which I had also brought with me, and did not use much on the trip. We drove onto our accommodation, consisting of a number of very smart Bandas with full facilities, including mosquito nets over the beds.

The garden was filled with flowers, which also bordered the path leading up to the Communal Centre, where we ate our meals. I decided to freshen up before exploring the site.

The lunch was excellent. I started with soup, and followed it with a salad with an avocado pear sauce. The main course was Nile Perch, followed by a coconut cake to finish off the meal. I was not keen on coconut, but after the morning we had had it tasted lovely. I then went back to the Banda to sort out my bag before the walk around Lake Duluti which was scheduled for four o'clock.

It was ten to four when I set off to meet up with the other nine in the Group, who had decided to go for the walk.

We walked along the roadway and down a track, passed a small hotel. The hotel was covered with Bougainvillea which was in full flower. We then came to a banana plantation on the one side, and a field full of ripening coffee plants on the other. The forest around the lake looked thick and lush, typical of an African equatorial rain forest. It was quite dark in the forest, but we could still see the birds. Just above me on the branch of a tree was a Squirrel, dashing across to the next tree. Thick vines hung down, the sort you see in Tarzan films, and it made me feel like swinging from them. The trees themselves were tall, some up to a hundred feet. We were half a mile into the walk and it was hot and humid, so we stopped to have a drink and take photos of the birds we could see. I took one of a Fish Eagle, and a couple of the Lake. We could see several types of small birds and Paul, the Chairman of the Birdwatching Group, pointed out a Paradise Flycatcher to me. I could see its long tail plumage and vibrant colours. It clearly was a stunning sight.

Figure 33 Paradise Flycatcher

The lake walk was approximately three miles long, and took us about two hours to complete. About halfway around, the forest was thicker, with bamboo sticking out into the lake. Strange noises filled the air, made by insects we could not see. The insects, which we could see, were mainly brightly coloured Butterflies, and there were thousands of ants running up and down the path. A large blue and yellow Swallowtail Butterfly fluttered past, as we reached the halfway stage. On a branch jutting out of the lake, a couple of White-chested Cormorants sat side by side. I tried to photograph them without disturbing them but, unfortunately, the light was in front of me.

As we went further around the lake, we came to an area where the bank had a steep drop. The local people had erected a branch and twig walkway, to enable people to circumvent the lake. Two thirds of the way around the lake, the view was even better. I could see a Heron perched in a tree, but it flew off before I could take my camera out. However, I took a wonderful photograph of the reflection of Mount Meru in the water.

I was soaking wet with perspiration, although the light was fading because we were out of the sun. It was definitely cooler. Even so, the high humidity still existed. Around the edge of the lake the water was clear, and I saw fish ranging in size up to a foot in length. I wished I had brought my fishing rod with me, because I had never seen so many fish in one place. Brightly coloured Dragonflies zipped around us. As we left the lakeside and entered the coffee plantation again, we could see the Lodge up on the hillside. The Bandas were purpose-built with thatched rooves. The Group posed for a photo before we re-entered the Lodge.

That evening we had a farewell dinner where we said our goodbyes to each other. I did not think I would see any of the group again, so I was pleased they had shared their great adventure with me. The meal consisted of delicious fish, which came from Lake Victoria, accompanied by potatoes and vegetables. It was another tasty meal, and I enjoyed it together with a lager or two!

Figure 34 Award token

After the meal, we had a presentation of Awards. I was presented with one by Paul, the Chairman of the Birdwatching Group, for my portrayal of "Moby Dick" in the swimming pool in Tarangire. I realized they were "extracting the Michael", but it was all in good humour, and made us all laugh. It was actually a small cardboard shield from a golf bag, but it was something that made me feel accepted by the group of complete strangers, and something I would treasure. I went back to my Banda to pack my bag before retiring to bed, as we were setting off quite early in the morning. I felt quite shattered.

Chapter 20

Homeward Bound

We were up at five o'clock next morning, because we were heading for the airport, and homeward bound. In fact, we were originally woken up just after three o'clock, because the coach driver thought that was the time we were due to go to the airport. He then realized he was two hours too early!! I did not feel like eating a large breakfast, so I had tea and toast instead. I felt as if my stomach upset had returned, but it could have been "flying nerves". More likely, the lager last night at the farewell dinner. My stomach had settled as we set off for the Airport. Along the way the views of Kilimanjaro were stunning. There was only a small amount of cloud on one side, leaving the snow-capped summit quite clear.

Luckily, as we boarded the aeroplane at Kilimanjaro airport, I was able to get a window seat on the left-hand side of the plane, facing the terminal building. Consequently, I was able to get good views of the building and the top of Kilimanjaro, as we took off and banked around the summit, before we headed over Kenya. By the time we were over the summit of Mount Kilimanjaro, we were above eighteen thousand feet, giving me an excellent view of the crater on top and enabling me to take a photo.

It was not long before we were over Nairobi, and I could see the ground clearly with different shades of green, the buildings, and an enormous lake north of the city. We crossed the Equator, and continued over Lake Turkana in Northern Kenya, prior to flying on to Addis. I could see the lake clearly, although we were at full altitude. The ground looked brown, with some greenery around the lake's edges. The lake itself was quite green.

This had truly been a wonderful Adventure that I will never forget.

Lightning Source UK Ltd.
Milton Keynes UK
UKHW020814031121
393262UK00008B/87